Discover

North Norfolk

Maps. Ordnance Survey maps 132, 133 and 134 of the Landranger series cover north Norfolk at a scale of 1:50,000, approximately 1.25 inches to 1 mile.

Notes for foreign readers. Before decimalisation in 1971, British currency had 12 pennies or pence to a shilling, and 20 shillings to a pound. Six shillings and eightpence was written either 6s 8d or 6/8d and was worth 33p in decimal terms. **B&B** means 'bed and breakfast,' usually available in private houses, farmhouses or pubs (public houses). You will see the sign all over the country and in this book. American readers should note that their 'first floor' is the British **ground floor,** their second the British first.

General notes. Admission fees and opening hours are correct at the time of research but are subject to change. The fee quoted is for one adult and ignores concessions for children, senior citizens, groups, etc.

◀Cover: the east beach at Cromer.

Discover

North

Norfolk

Terry Palmer

HERITAGE
HOUSE

DISCOVER NORTH NORFOLK

First published April 1992

ISBN 1.85215.0351

Typesetting by Anglia Photoset, Colchester, from in-house computer setting. Typeface is Rockwell, 8.5 on 9.5.

Printed by Colorcraft, Hong Kong.

Distributed by Heritage House at 'Lavandou,' Steam Mill Rd, Bradfield, Manningtree, CO11 2QT, ✆0255.870595.

Published by Heritage House (Publishers) Ltd, King's Rd, Clacton-on-Sea, Essex, CO15 1BG.

Acknowledgements. Michael Barrett, head of history, Gresham School, Holt; David Case, Wells Harbour Commissioners; Denis Condon, Worstead; Lt Cmdr Francis, Wells & Walsingham Railway; Frances Hoyo, South Gate, King's Lynn; Jim Jordan, Swaffham; Lorraine Marshall, Wells Harbourmaster's Office; Mark Regan, bellringer, St Mary-le-Bow, Whitechapel; Graham Walker, Wells Harbourmaster's Office; Dr Wells, Heacham; Whitechapel Bell Foundry; Les Winter, Burnham Thorpe.

Opinions expressed in this book are the author's except where stated otherwise.

Worldwide travel titles in the *Discover* series in print or in preparation include:

Cyprus & North Cyprus, The Dominican Republic, Florida, The Gambia, Gibraltar, The Grand Canyon State, Hungary, Malta, Morocco, Poland, Sardinia, Seychelles, Tunisia. (These titles are distributed to the book trade through Roger Lascelles, 47 York Rd, Brentford, TW8 OQP).

Titles on English regions akin to this volume: *Discover The Lower Stour* (Constable's Country, first published in 1975); *Discover The Suffolk Coast* (first published 1976, both republished in this format 1992); *Discover Norwich and the Broads.*

CONTENTS

MAPS

Terry Palmer (right) and Dennis Hawes get together again.

Terry Palmer was born on the Cambridgeshire-Norfolk border and moved to Essex in 1970. He has had a lifelong interest in writing, photography, maps, languages and travel, making him a perfect candidate for the role of travel writer. He was a reporter on the *Harwich and Manningtree Standard* in 1975 when Dennis Hawes suggested to him that 'somebody' should write a guide book to Manningtree. Terry and Dennis, with others, wrote and published the book themselves, and saw it top the local best-seller lists for several weeks.

Terry eventually moved on, via the Post Office trade paper, to establish his own publishing company, Heritage House, through which he publishes guides to far-flung destinations.

The story comes full circle as Dennis and Terry get together again to write and publish these regional guides to East Anglia.

1: STEP BACK IN TIME

A Norfolk overview – with railway history

NORFOLK IS A FASCINATING COUNTY. One of the driest parts of Britain, it has Broadland at its east and the now-drained Fenland at its west, with the dry sands of Breckland on its southern flank.

It is among the lowest counties of Britain – the highest point is Brink Hill between Gayton and Gt Massingham, which is 305ft (93m) above sea level – but it certainly is not flat. A ridge of chalk, topped locally with **carrstone,** a sandstone with a high iron content, runs south from Hunstanton's coloured cliffs to join Newmarket Heath and eventually become the Chiltern Hills; east of that the gently rolling landscape, including the optimistically-named 'High Norfolk,' has good if not rich farmland, with soils brought down during the Ice Age from far to the north; the hills behind Cromer and Sheringham are terminal moraines, the final dumping-ground of the glaciers before they retreated to Greenland and Iceland.

Coast and country. North Norfolk has a beautiful, unspoiled coastline, where the main road is still a country lane, and where the pressures of city life are forgotten. In summer the countryside grows corn, sugar beet, oilseed rape and flax (linseed) – these last two give the acres of early-season yellow flowers that you might confuse with mustard, and the later-blooming fields of pale blue. You can still find sheep on the rougher land and cattle on the marshes around the Broads, but East Anglia has long ceased to produce wool by the cartload and the shipload, as it did in the Middle Ages – although the village of Worsted is a living reminder of the worstead once woven there.

But in midwinter it can be bleak, when an icy wind scythes down from the Arctic. Don't forget – there is no land between here and the North Pole, and beyond that lies the barren coast of Siberia.

Norfolk worthies. The county has strong royal connections, particularly at **Sandringham** and at nearby King's Lynn, while in the east Blickling was the home of **Anne Boleyn.** Norfolk also gave us **Robert Walpole,** who created the job of Prime Minister; **Thomas Edward Coke** and **'Turnip' Townshend** who both revolutionised farming; and **Horatio Nelson** who became one of the country's greatest admirals.

Norfolk, indeed, has always been a maritime county, although the North Sea has treated it harshly. You can draw a map of the coast from Sheringham to Great Yarmouth with a single sweep of the pen, showing where the sea is still grinding away at the land; yet to the west the water is in retreat, as Blakeney Point and Scolt Head continue to grow, and as The Wash continues to silt up.

CHURCHES

For many visitors, Norfolk is a county of churches, each one the focal point of a bustling village in the days of the wool trade, when Norfolk had the densest population of any rural part of Britain and was England's richest county. The dying cloth industry decimated many villages, but their churches remain. Most are early medieval, often the size of a small cathedral, and almost all stand on the site of churches built before the Norman Conquest. Indeed, 119 of the county's surviving churches have round towers, a mark of their Saxon origins although some were built in Norman times. There are 41 round towers in Suffolk, and only 14 in the remainder of Britain.

The village church is such a vital part of every Norfolk community that no serious visitor should ignore this unique heritage. And to help you in your tour of discovery, here are some points to watch for:

The **tower** evolved as a place to hang the bell which called people to church in the times before clocks, but some early towers were also places of refuge against marauders, landmarks for fishermen, and perhaps storehouses for grain. It is difficult to find anywhere in Norfolk that is out of sight of a church tower, and from several high spots you can see at least half a dozen.

The **nave** is the main part of the church interior, its roof often looking like an upturned boat, hence the *naval* link. It is invariably lined east-west and almost always with the tower at the western end; on rare occasions the tower is partly offset, and on even rarer occasions it is freestanding. Most churches have a **chapel** at the east end of the nave; before the 16th-cent Reformation when Henry VIII took the Church from Catholicism to Protestantism, and Orthodoxy went its own way, the building and maintenance of the chapel was the priest's responsibility, and he often had his own private door into it. The churchwardens were responsible for the nave and tower.

Between nave and chapel was the **rood beam,** a sturdy timber 10ft to 15ft (3m to 5m) up, supporting the ornately-worked **rood screen.** The **rood** itself was the carving of the crucified Christ, usually fixed in the middle of the beam and the subject of medieval oaths when people swore 'by the Rood.' No church kept its rood after the Reformation, but a very few still have traces of the rood stair, set into the outer wall.

It was normal practise for parishioners to enter church through the **south porch,** located on the sunny side, while the door in the **north porch** was kept ajar during baptisms so the Devil could make his escape as another soul was dedicated to Christ. Modern road systems sometimes make the north porch the more convenient in these less-superstitious times, but of the county's 660 churches, 468 use the south door, 152 opt for the north, while 40 have a west door, usually through the tower.

The **east window** is the main source of light above the high altar, and is usually a dominant part of the church, well worth a closer look.

Even tombs have their messages in code. A man whose arms or legs are crossed had been on a Crusade to the Holy Land, but a man or woman whose feet rested on a little dog had died peacefully in bed.

Churches had to be built of local material, but good stone is rare in Norfolk. The Saxons worked solely in flint, which dictated the round tower, as you cannot build a 90° corner in this stone. After the Norman Conquest, cornerstones were shipped in from Normandy, which was more convenient than hauling them overland from Leicester, but flint was still the main building material except in the north-west of the county where carrstone provided a suitable and colourful alternative.

Stately **yew trees** have been planted in English churchyards almost since the coming of Christianity, but we are only now beginning to appreciate that many are 1,200 years old and to learn their symbolism; the location of an ancient yew in a churchyard can show us where the original Saxon or early Norman church was built, even if no trace remains.

This is one of the surviving fords in Norfolk, but it's useful for cleaning all makes of car.

RAILWAYS

Norfolk had a good rail network at nationalisation in 1948, but economies and line closures have hit the county badly. The **Great Eastern** had a main line from Liverpool St, London, serving King's Lynn and Hunstanton, with a branch line from Lynn to Swaffham, East Dereham, Wymondham and Norwich; and another branch from Heacham to Wells, Fakenham and on to Dereham. There was a further loop from Dereham through North Elmham and Aylsham to Wroxham, where it met the Norwich to Cromer line, while another track ran from Norwich, due east through Acle, to Great Yarmouth Vauxhall.

The **Midland and Great Northern Joint Railway,** the old M&GN, the 'muddle and get nowhere,' ran from Wisbech North to Lynn, sharing the station there with the GE, then on to Fakenham, Melton Constable, Aylsham, and Great Yarmouth Beach; there were branch lines from Melton Constable to Norwich; and to Holt, Sheringham and Cromer: a tiny stretch of this route survives as the **Poppy Line,** run by steam enthusiasts.

Lynn & Dereham. The Lynn & Dereham Line, incorporated in 1845 with £270,000 capital, was a continuation of the Lynn & Ely and the two soon became the **East Anglian Railway.** The double-track line to Narborough opened on 27 October 1846, and reached Swaffham on 10 August 1847. It struggled the few miles to Sporle by 26 October, and reached destination at East Dereham on 11 September 1848.

The L&D had encountered major problems: the high cost of land and the difficulty in cutting through the chalk at Swaffham, sent the cost of laying the double track to £24,000 per mile (£15,000 per km) and bankrupted the contractors.

By 1897 it was running eight services daily, which rose to nine in 1914, and its peak of 12 a day in 1955, using diesel cars. From 1900 to 1914 it took coaches from Doncaster through to Yarmouth, tacked on at March (Cambs), and in the short years from 1916 to 1921 it also added coaches from York.

In 1961 the service was down to nine local diesel cars daily; April 1966 saw the abandoning of all freight services except the movement of sand from Middletown Towers near Lynn; in August of that year all the stations became unmanned, with passengers paying on the train, but on 9 September 1968 the line closed: its daily passenger load was down to 700, its annual revenue just £22,000, but its operational cost was £46,000.

The EAR had a companion in the **Norfolk Railway** which carved a track from Norwich through Wymondham (pronounced *Windam*) to Dereham. Authorised in 1845, it was hauling freight from 7 December 1846 and passengers from 15 February 1847.

Before the line was complete its operators had won approval for an extension from Dereham to Wells and Blakeney, but it got no further than Fakenham, opening for service on 20 March 1849. The route was completed by the **Wells & Fakenham Railway,** incorporated in 1854 with the Earl of Leicester, owner of Holkham Hall, investing £10,000, the town of Wells contributing £14,000, and directors of the Norfolk Railway, acting as individuals, providing £30,000. The line opened on 1 December 1857, which was declared a local public holiday, with the extension to Wells Harbour coming in 1859.

In 1862 the W&F was absorbed by the GER, and by 1892 the town of Wells had a daily through coach to Liverpool St. Silting of the harbour brought a decline in goods traffic, but day trippers came in their hundreds from Norwich, and the line brought many pilgrims to Walsingham.

In decline, the Wells to Heacham line was a victim of the East Coast Floods of January 1953, and the Wells-Fakenham route closed for passengers on 5 October 1964. On the last day of the month freight traffic ceased for Wells, and by January 1983 the line ran no further than North Elmham; this spur closed in January 1989.

The **Lynn & Fakenham Railway** opened its Gaywood to Massingham track on 16 August 1879, and extended it to Fakenham a year later, to the day, using three locomotives from the Cornish Railway. The M&GN bought the line in 1893 and did reasonable business moving cereals, sugar beet and livestock, but human passengers were never profitable. The line was at its busiest around the 1930s, and carried 571 trainloads of aviation fuel to RAF bases during World War Two but, after the war, traffic declined as road transport improved. The passenger service ceased on 2 March 1959, and freight on 1 May 1968.

Thelmethorpe Curve. The GER's Wroxham to Dereham line ran parallel with the M&GN's Cromer to Norwich line for a mile, near the village of Thelmethorpe, after the former went under a bridge carrying the latter. When both lines were facing closure, British Rail abandoned the bridge and joined the lines with the Thelmethorpe Curve, 518 yards (472m) of track that opened on 12 September 1960 but closed to passengers in February 1969 and to goods in January 1982.

Lynn & Hunstanton. The single-track Lynn & Hunstanton Railway opened on 3 October in 1862, the year that the Prince of Wales bought Sandringham House. Hunstanton had less than 500 people in the 1861 census, and was just beginning to become fashionable as a select resort; within a decade the population had doubled. The fishermen using Snettisham's deepwater port sent their catches to market by rail, joining the grain, cattle, manure and coal which formed the freight traffic.

The L'Estrange family, the main landowner in Hunstanton, gave most of the ground needed for the line, which was therefore built at a cost of less than £60,000. The GER operated the line for 50% of the takings, plus £10 per track mile per week – but the L&HR had to pay £10,000 compensation for an accident on 3 August 1863 when the train hit a bull. Seven people, as well as the bull, were killed, with almost 20 severely injured.

In 1874 the L&HR merged with the West Norfolk Junction Railway, and the two were swallowed by the GER on 1 July 1890. The GER doubled the track from Lynn to Wolferton by 1899, in view of the Royal traffic on the line, with the Prince of Wales paying for **Wolferton Station;** the remainder of the line remained single-track.

By 1900 there were 12 trains daily each way in summer, six in winter, with connections to Liverpool Street in 187 minutes and to St Pancras in 184. In 1905 a Sunday restaurant car was added for the use of golfers.

The railways had started a major social revolution in rural Britain, with the scattered population of the eastern counties being among the greatest beneficiaries: never before had so many people been able to afford the luxury of travel. In the summer of 1922 there were 14 trains daily each way, Mon-Fri, between Lynn and Hunstanton, with extra Sunday excursions.

Traffic was severely reduced during World War Two, but I remember my first ever postwar rail journey, from Wisbech to Hunstanton on a sunny Sunday, in a crowded train: in those days nobody minded having to stand. A few years later I was on my first car

West Walton Church in the Fens west of King's Lynn, has a tower separate from the nave. But so has Little Snoring on page 94.

journey to Hunstanton, with the homeward traffic queueing from Sandringham to get through the bottleneck of King's Lynn. In those days even traffic jams were a new experience – but they signalled the end of the railway.

Drama in the floods. There was drama on the line during the East Coast Floods of 1953. On 31 January the 1927 down train was caught in the high tide north of Heacham; a floating bungalow hit the smoke stack, damaged the vacuum brakes, and put the fire out. The disabled train stood motionless for six hours, with the floodwaters reaching seat level. As the tide receded the footplate crew repaired the brakes, used the floor from the tender as fuel, and crawled back to Hunstanton. So many chalets and beach huts had been washed onto the line that it was blocked until 23 February.

Despite all endeavours, the line was dying. Diesel cars were introduced in 1958, but on summer Sundays in 1966 there were only two excursions from Liverpool St to Hunstanton, and they ceased forever at the season's end.

From 1967 British Rail operated the line as a self-contained business. Stations were unmanned, and there was one platform at Hunstanton. Level crossing gates went, replaced by the first automatic barriers in the country, and all signalling was controlled from Lynn. BR cut the line's running costs from £100,000 a year to £35,000, but the income of £40,000 also slumped, and the line was closed on 5 May 1969.

Economists now say that it was wrong to expect every branch line to pay its way; a branch that ran at a loss would bring extra revenue to a main line already working at a profit; cut the branch and you starve the main line.

Heacham to Wells. The West Norfolk Junction Railway opened the Heacham to Wells line on 17 August 1866, although the Prince and Princess of Wales had been taken to Holkham by rail on 13 January. The GER operated the line on a partnership, and took it over on 1 July 1890. Its passenger service was an early victim to changing circumstances, closing on 2 June 1952. The Burnham Market to Wells section was damaged in the 1953 floods, and abandoned; the freight service on the section to Heacham survived until 28 December 1964.

East Norfolk Railway. The East Norfolk Railway, incorporated in 1864, began work on the Whitlingham Junction (Norwich) to North Walsham line in 1865, but stopped when the contractor died and his assets were frozen. Work resumed in 1870, and in 1872 the ENR had Parliamentary approval to extend the track to Cromer – but Cromer didn't want the railway.

A single track opened to North Walsham on 20 October 1874, to Gunton on 29 July 1876 and, despite the objections, opening at Cromer on 26 March 1877.

The GER took control in 1881 and between 1896 and 1900 doubled the track to North Walsham. The first trains were slow, coming from Liverpool St to Cromer in 310 minutes, but on 1 July 1897 the daily summer-only *Cromer Express* did the journey, non-stop to North Walsham, in 175 minutes. Renamed the *Norfolk Coast Express* with 12 coaches, this was the pride of the GER until it ceased running in 1914, and a revival after WW2 saw the *Norfolkman* and the *Broadsman* operate for several years. Then on 18 June 1985 the Post Office chartered the *Orient Express* to come to Cromer and promote the Safety at Sea stamp issue, the first time the luxury train had entered the eastern counties. It was possible only because Cromer, the resort which didn't want the railway, is – with Sheringham – now the only one on the north Norfolk coast still to be served by rail.

FOOTPATHS

Norfolk does not have a great amount of public footpaths and bridleways, mainly because it has a very comprehensive network of country lanes, a relic of Medieval times when the county had a much denser rural population. Motor traffic is light on most of the lanes, but the passing of occasional cars has obvious disadvantages.

Among the major paths are the **Peddar's Way,** coming up from mid-Suffolk and hitting the coast at Holme next the Sea near Hunstanton. It was straight when built by the Romans after the defeat of the Iceni under Queen Boadicea (Boudicca) in 61AD, and there was probably a ferry crossing The Wash to join the roads to Lincoln and York. The modern Peddar's Way uses footpaths, bridleways and country lanes, and goes through only one village, Castle Acre.

At Holme it meets the **Norfolk Coast Path,** meandering from Hunstanton to Cromer along some splendid if undramatic coastal scenery and past several nature reserves. At Cromer the recently-designated **Weavers' Way** begins, taking walkers on a circuitous route through Aylsham, North Walsham, Stalham and Acle, to Great Yarmouth, following parts of the old M&GN railway line. And from Yarmouth the **Angles Way,** also known as the **Waveney Way,** traces the river's course to its source west of Diss, then continues downstream along the Little Ouse River until it meets the Peddar's Way.

The **Peddars Way Association** at 150 Armes St, Norwich NR2 4EG (✆0603.623070) publishes a guide and accommodation list on the Peddars Way and Norfolk Coast Path, and a separate one on the Angles Way, each at £1.65 plus 24p postage.

NATURE RESERVES

The Norfolk Naturalists Trust (72 Cathedral Close, Norwich NR1 4DF, ✆0603.625540) has 14 nature reserves, and the Royal Society for

14

the Protection of Birds (RSPB, The Lodge, Sandy, Beds, SG19 2DL) has two, both marked on OS Landranger maps. Taken west to east, those in north Norfolk are:

Roydon Common, 3 miles NE of Lynn on A148 then signposted south. Sandy heath and wetlands; vital for specialist plants; insects, including dragonfly; birds. Always open.

Narborough Railway Line, 1 mile south of Narborough, SE of Lynn; disused railway embankment has rich chalk-grassland community, good for butterflies. Always open.

Snettisham, RSPB reserve with hides. Common tern nest site with summer visiting ducks; shingle flora. Always open; signposted from Snettisham. Details, ✆0485.42689.

Holme Dunes, north of A149 at Holme next the Sea; habitats include saltmarsh, dune, wetlands. Excellent spot during bird migrations, with 280 species recorded. Open daily 1000-1700, fee.

Titchwell Marsh, RSPB reserve with hides; ringed plover, ruff, dunlin are common; black tern, kingfisher and others frequent. At low tide, remains of a **petrified forest** visible. Many shell varieties found here. Shop, WC, picnic site. ✆0485.210779.

Scolt Head Island – see chapter 3.

Cley Marshes, major birdwatching site, with more than 300 species seen, including many rarities. Hides, including ♿ access. Open Tues-Sun, Apr-Oct 1000-1700, fee.

Foxley Wood, 2 miles north of Bawdeswell and near Thelmethorpe Curve (see 'railways'); the county's largest stand of ancient woodland; butterflies and wild flowers. Open year round Fri-Wed 1000-1700.

FISHING

Sea fishing. There is limited scope for sea fishing from the shore, but at Cromer try the third breakwater east of the pier on the last half of the flood tide, or the pier itself, from where you may catch mackerel on calm evenings. Beach fishing is possible at **Weybourne, Sheringham,** where cod up to 18lb (8kg) have been caught, and from **Trimingham** to **Mundesley.**

Freshwater fishing. Try the 25-acre **Blickling Lake,** the lake on the **Holkham Estate,** and at **Letheringsett,** near Holt; permits and permission required. There's also a trout fishery at **Reepham,** ✆0603.870878, with fish up to 15lb (7kg).

You know it already, but *please do not use lead weights.*

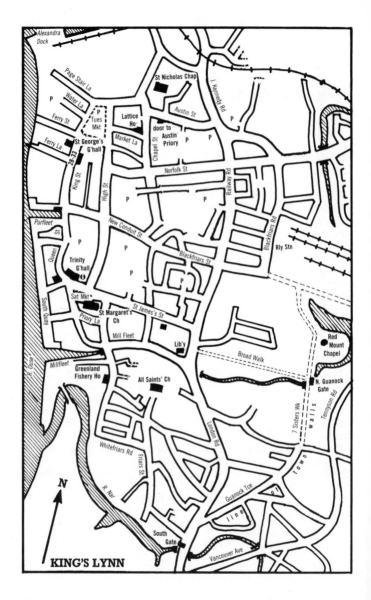

KING'S LYNN

2: KING'S LYNN

Royal Norfolk

BEFORE 1537, KING'S LYNN was called 'Bishop's Lynn.' The bishop in question was Herbert de Losinga who in 1094 paid William II at least 1,000 marks (£666) for the office and title of Bishop of Norwich.

When Norwich Cathedral was consecrated in 1101, Pope Paschal II learned of the bribe, which was as much a crime then as now, and he ordered the bishop to build more priories and churches in his diocese as penance. The main ones were at **Great Yarmouth,** built on a sandbank and long since lost; and the church of *Holy Mary Magdalene and St Margaret, and All Holy Virgins.* The latter, now known as St Margaret's, was built on a saltmarsh on Losinga's own lands in the west of the county at the settlement called Linn, from the Saxon word for a small lake. Linn, which already had the Saxon church of All Hallows, took the name of 'Bishop Losinga,' later reverting to Bishop's Lynn, with its new Saturday market beside St Margaret's Church.

Bishop Turbe of Norwich (1146-74) was not to be outsmarted by Losinga, so he built his own town a mile or so to the north, gave it the Church of St Nicholas – it was the Chapel of Ease for Losinga's St Margaret's – and endowed it with another market, to be held on Tuesday.

Two towns. We therefore had *two* towns, evolving separately until King John granted the Royal Charter in 1204 which united them. Medieval markets could not survive without royal approval, and John was magnanimous in allowing both to thrive, which is why King's Lynn still has two markets to this day.

Turbe's town was designed on the grid system, with plots of equal size and commanding equal rents, all of which was recorded in a plan drawn in the 13th cent and which is still in existence.

When the plan was compiled, Turbe's part of town was more important than Losinga's so almost all the plots were taken and the black-robed Augustinian friars, reorganised in the 12th cent, were lucky to find a site near Tuesday Market; their friary is remembered in the name of Austin Street, where the doorway stands as a sole remnant.

Other friars. The Dominicans, also known as the Black Friars from the black hood worn over their white cloak; the Fransiscans or Grey Friars; and the Carmelites or White Friars: all were obliged to find plots to the south of town. **Greyfriars Tower** in Tower Gardens near the library, is the only part of the 15th-cent priory to survive the dissolution of the monasteries; an archway of the 12th-cent **Benedictine Priory** stands in Priory Lane, south of St Margaret's Church; while Blackfriars St near the museum, and Whitefriars Rd near Friars Fleet – the River Nar by the South Gate – mark the sites of the other religious orders.

The Benedictines of St Margaret's Church had rights over the income from the Saturday Market until Bishop John de Grey of Norwich took them over in 1205. The Carmelites of St Mary's Church were vegetarians, never spoke a word, and slept in their own coffins. The Austins had an altar called the 'stairway to Heaven' in their church, and they sang Mass over their dead. The Dominicans survived the burning of their priory in 1486, at a time when Lynn had more than 70 religious orders; they escaped the dissolution of the monasteries, and stayed in town until 1845.

Massacre of the Jews. Followers of other religions found life somewhat harder. For example, Surrey St, at the south-east corner of Tuesday Market, began life as Jews' Lane, but no trace of their homes remains. Many Jews were massacred here, as elsewhere in England, in January 1189 in the celebrations which marked preparations for Richard I's departure on the Third Crusade to the Holy Land, ironically the Jewish homeland.

Millfleet. 'Fleet' is an old word meaning 'shallow,' and in Lynn it means a shallow river. The Millfleet, just north of Friars Fleet, was bridged in 1250, linking Bishop's Lynn with the independent village of South Lynn. The Purfleet, the town's main port until recent times, marked the vague division between Losinga's community and Turbe's settlement, with the Fisher Fleet, near the present Alexandra Dock, forming a boundary to the north.

Bishop's Lynn prospered from its monastic ties, but its location at the mouth of the Great Ouse, sheltered from storms although endowed with a strong tide and perpetually prone to flooding, turned its people's thoughts towards maritime trade. From the earliest recorded times, ships were sailing from Lynn around the English coast and across to the Low Countries and Saxony. An example of this trade shows after the Great Fire of 1331 which destroyed many of Lynn's houses, built of daub and wattle walls (mud spread over thin branches of hazelwood) between cornerposts of heavy oak, and roofed with thatch. After the fire the burghers demanded more brick and tile, but these were more expensive than softwood from the Baltic and Norfolk's own reeds.

The Guild of Holy Trinity in King's Lynn is one of the oldest in the country as well as being one of the most distinctive.

GUILDHALLS

The **Guild of St George,** which was founded in 1376 and met in the late-13th-cent hall of the Holy Trinity, received its charter from Henry IV in 1406. The old hall had escaped the fire of 1331 but the guildsmen, wanting a new home, built it between 1410 and 1420 on King St, near Tuesday Market. It is an unassuming place with a brick facing wall, broken by a large window with six main lights, but as World War Two bombing damaged the guildhalls of London and York, St George's in Lynn is the oldest surviving medieval guildhall in England. Owned by the National Trust, it is now home to a theatre, art exhibitions, and the **King's Lynn Festival** in summer.

By contrast, **Trinity Guildhall** at the north-west corner of Saturday Market, was built in 1421, a year after St George's was completed, and its unusual façade of alternating blocks of pale limestone and dark flint give it the appearance of a chequerboard and make it one of the most-photographed guildhalls in East Anglia.

Both guilds used the undercroft – the cellars – to store their wine, among other things, while feasting and revelry went on in the main hall. Medieval guilds fulfilled a strange role, combining town council, tradesmen's federation, benevolent society, bank, and early trade union, usually with religious overtones. This was too powerful a mixture for Edward VI, so in 1547 he disbanded all guilds and in many cases seized their assets for the crown; after all, his father Henry VIII had dissolved the monasteries in 1536 and '37, and the friaries in 1538.

Indeed, it had been Henry VIII's disagreements with the established Catholic Church over his divorce from Catherine of Aragon in 1521, which prompted the town to change its name from the politically-sensitive Bishop's Lynn to King's Lynn in 1537.

Jailhouse. In 1571, therefore, with the timber floor of the main hall replaced by brick barrel-vaulting, still clearly visible from below, the cellars became a prison. Surprisingly, they continued in this role, with only minor variations, until 1937.

King John Cup. Trinity Guildhall and its cellars were restored in the 1950s and the undercroft is now used as a museum holding some priceless treasures, notably the silver **King John Cup,** the oldest known secular loving cup in England, made around 1340 in the reign of Edward III, not of John. The **King John Sword** has Latin engravings which translate *this sword was given by King John from his own side* and *Long Live King Henry VIII in the 20th year of his reign,* but the weapon is probably Tudor. King John's charter of 1204, on parchment, is definitely original and is on display with later charters, and the **Red Register,** used throughout the 14th cent to record wills and deeds; this is one of the oldest paper books in the world.

You will also see the **Nuremberg Cup** which Thomas Soone, three times mayor, presented to the town in 1634; the modern mayoral chain of office; the seal of the Guild of St George; and a tankard given to Samuel Gurney Cresswell in 1853. Samuel, born in Lynn, is credited locally as being the first man to complete the North-West Passage, the sea route north of Canada – but other authorities give this honour to Roald Amundsen in 1903-05.

King John's jewels. You will not see the legendary jewels which King John supposedly lost in The Wash. This incident happened on the low-tide crossing between Walpole Cross Keys and Sutton Bridge (Lincolnshire), near the route of the modern A17, as in John's reign (1199-1216) The Wash extended inland to Wisbech. You can still see traces of the Roman sea wall from Holbeach to Long Sutton, and from Cross Keys to West Lynn.

The Regalia Rooms are open May-Oct Mon-Sat 1000-1600, Sun 1000-1500; Nov-Apr Fri-Sat 1000-1600, 50p; access from the neighbouring **Town Hall,** built in similar flint and limestone style in 1895. The **Tourist Office** is in the old **Jail House,** built in 1784 and in use as a police station until 1935; you can have a quick look in the cells. The tourist office is open Mon-Thur 0900-1700, Fri-Sat 0915-1630, Sun 1000-1500.

Ouse reclaimed. While The Wash in Norman times extended inland to Wisbech, so the Great Ouse river flowed along a different channel. Its waters were several miles wide and swept in a big bend from Wiggenhall St German in the south, out into the Fens before

King's Lynn South Gates is the most impressive remnant of medieval town wall in East Anglia, because traffic continues to use it.

flowing through the narrow gap between Clenchwarton and Lynn. In the 14th and 15th cents some of the river bed was reclaimed, but the present course was cut in 1853, straightening and narrowing the river. **Thoresby College** in Queen St has a slate marking the site of the quay around 1300, showing that the present quayside is also on reclaimed land. The college, by the way, was founded by the merchant Thomas Thoresby for teaching 16 priests, and is now a **Youth Hostel;** ✆0553.763871 for an appointment to view its Great Hall.

REBUILDING THE TOWN

The town itself was gradually rebuilt between 1550 and 1650 in brick, fired in kilns at Gaywood and West Lynn using local clay. Lynn Corporation bought these bricks at £5 per 1,000 in 1613, which was phenominally expensive as in 1437 it had bought 200,000 bricks for the South Gate (see below) for just £50, and my father, building in Wisbech in 1934, paid only £1.50 per 1,000.

With the ever-present fear of fire, thatch was forbidden within the town, so roofing tiles were shipped in from the Netherlands. This was easy as Lynn was already a major trading port, as shown by the **Hanseatic Warehouse** near the river, built in the 1480s by and for German merchants and their goods on land provided by Edward IV. Marriott's Barn, standing parallel to the river, has stone walls to withstand the occasional high tide, its timber upper structure probably being 16th-cent German work.

The warehouse was renamed St Margaret's House after a local man, Edward Everard, bought it in 1751 for St Margaret's Church. And the Hanseatic League? That was a medieval protection society for merchants trading abroad, and covered Cologne, Lübeck and Hamburg, with Bremen a later member. It disintegrated during the Thirty Years' War, 1618-48.

Custom House. The **Greenland Fishery** building in Bridge St was added in 1605, made of timber but with brick gables, but the most architecturally outstanding addition was the Customs House, financed by Charles Turner of Warham but designed and built in 1683 by Henry Bell, a local man responsible for several constructions in the town, although this was his greatest achievement, a classical concept long before its time. The building, on the north side of the Purfleet, has on its south wall sculpted heads wearing corn ears and grapes, symbols of the trade out and into the port. The house is listed for preservation and is not open to the public.

As I write, the near-derelict schooner *Dania* sits on the Purfleet mud. The vessel was used in the film *Revolution,* a box-office disaster which was shot in medieval Lynn.

Ferry. The next street to the north of Purfleet Quay is Ferry Lane, which leads to the passenger-only ferry operating the half-hour service across to West Lynn and its canning factories. The fare is 30p.

THE TOWN WALLS

Bishop's Lynn had been well-defended since its beginning, at its south by Friar's Fleet (also known as the River Nar by outsiders, the River Esk by townspeople, or the Puny River by people from Middleton, 5 miles (8km) south-east), at its west by the main river, and in the north by the Purfleet and the Fisherfleet. That left only the landward approach from the east.

Back in 1294 Edward I had granted Lynn the right to levy *murage,* a tax on goods brought into town and used for financing the building of a defensive wall, a *mur* in Norman (and modern) French. The wall was mostly an earth embankment, but the gates, and parts protecting Turbe's New Town, were of stone. East Gate, demolished in 1800, stood on today's Littleport St near the railway station, and Dowshill Gate was near the present railway to Alexandra Dock; it has also gone.

South Gate. Two of the town's old gateways survive to this day, one being the much-restored and seldom-seen **North Guanock Gate** near the north-east end of Guanock Terrace, leading from the South Gate. The other is the South Gate itself, the most impressive medieval gateway in the eastern counties because much of the traffic entering the town centre from the south must pass through it, even today; its only rivals in Norfolk are the smaller portal at Castle Acre, and

Erpingham Gate in Norwich.

The present structure was built in 1437 of brick faced with stone, probably standing on the site of the gate built during the reign of Edward III (1327-77). Maintenance for that earlier work was the responsibility of the villages as far away as Castle Acre, Stoke Ferry, and Fordham near Downham Market, but the people of Lynn were responsible for the later structure, begun by Robert Hertanger, a mason from London who received his £100 fee in advance. Hertanger spent much of the money on drink, was sacked 'by reason of his poverty,' and the corporation hired another mason to finish the job.

In the Middle Ages it was the Gatekeeper's task to charge tolls on goods entering the town, to close the gates at dusk (there was never a drawbridge here) and, when bubonic plague was around, to keep out anybody who could not provide a good reason for entering the town. Robert Anthony, appointed as gatekeeper in 1509, was also 'cleanser of the muckhills,' as the town's rubbish was dumped just outside.

Later gatekeepers rented the building from the corporation and took a percentage of the tolls, although they no longer lived in the large first-floor room, but on 25 March 1723 the last keeper was ordered to quit the job as tolls were abolished on that day. The council still appoints a gatekeeper, but the role is purely honourary – except for Wednesdays Jun-Sep 1100-1500 when the keeper admits tourists to the gate, free.

The Honest Lawyer. Have you ever met an honest lawyer? There's one beside the South Gate, but it's a pub, its sign showing the lawyer carrying his head under his arm.

Civil War. None of Lynn's defences was tested in battle although the South Gate was threatened during the Civil War of 1642-49 when Royalists led by Sir Hamon L'Estrange of Hunstanton seized the town and were besieged by the Roundheads – Parliamentarians – under the Earl of Manchester from 28 August to 16 September 1643. After Lynn's dubious water supply was cut, the town surrendered.

Red Mount Chapel. The Red Mount Chapel was never part of the defences; indeed, it was in no-man's-land between the earth bank and the water-filled ditch. Built around 1485 by the friars, it supplemented their meagre income by offering lodging to pilgrims who had come by sea and were about to face the long trek across the county to Walsingham – and, of course, those pilgrims on their homeward journey. After the dissolution of the friaries in 1538 and the collapse of the Walsingham Pilgrimage, the Red Mount Chapel lost its customers, but managed to survive. It's still there today, an octagonal structure atop its small mound.

It's unusual to find old churches deviating from the traditional design, but Wisbech had its Octagon Church until the 1950s, and St

Sepulchre in Cambridge is otherwise known as the Round Church, one of five in the country.

WITCHCRAFT

Maggie Read's heart. Margaret Read had been burned at the stake in Tuesday Market in 1590, her heart bursting from her body and flying across the large market square. Look for a diamond-shaped brick with a heart carved on it, set high in a wall on the north-east corner of the market, showing where Maggie's heart stopped its flight. But another legend claims it bounced down Water Lane and into the river.

The crime of sorcery was punishable by hanging, but if a witch had used her so-called powers to kill anybody, then the penalty was death by fire.

Elizabeth Housegoe died at the stake in 1598, and Mary Smith followed in 1616. Mary had been accused of bewitching Elizabeth Hancocke, who fell ill and died after Mary had called "a pox to light on you." A witness for the prosecution was the Rev Mr Roberts who, in 1615, had laid a private water pipe to his house on Tuesday Market – the house that bore the mark of Maggie Read's heart.

Heresy. William Sawtré was burned to death at Smithfield, London, in 1401, not for witchcraft but for heresy. He has the distinction of being England's first martyr in the Church's campaign against disbelievers.

Charles Turner of Warham near Wells, built the Duke's Head inn on Tuesday Market around 1630, shortly before East Anglia was gripped in the worst persecution of witches, with Matthew Hopkins of Manninngtree, Essex, emerging as the self-appointed Witchfinder General. In 1646 Lynn Corporation sent for Hopkins, who duly earned his £5 fee by finding two witches and seeing them hang in Tuesday Market.

CAPTAIN VANCOUVER and the MARITIME CONNECTION

Lynn's 11th-cent seagoing merchants exported wool, fish, and salt from the town's saltpans, and brought back millstones, furs and cloth. A century later, merchants from Brughes and Ghent were trading regularly into the port, with wool and cloth becoming dominent as sheep-rearing made East Anglia the wealthiest part of the country.

Wine and wool. The abbeys of Ely, Peterborough, and the neighbouring villages of Ramsey and Crowland, sent vast consignments of wool out through Lynn, with sample records showing that in 1267 the town handled 1,406 sacks of it worth £3,440, a vast amount of money. In return, Lynn's merchants brought back increasing amounts of wine from Gascony, with Henry III ordering 50 tuns (1 tun = 252

The old Customs House on King's Lynn's Purfleet.

gallons = 1,145 litres) for Kenilworth Castle in 1266.

While ports on the Suffolk coast were concentrating on fishing, Lynn saw commerce as its main income. Gradually it increased its trading links, bringing in such exotic commodities as beeswax from Russia, timber from Finland, fish from Iceland – and pilgrims for Walsingham. By the early 17th cent, Lynn was almost as busy as Bristol, one of England's major ports of the time; in 1604 Lynn imported 96 shiploads of goods, and exported 159.

Smuggling was a major industry around the entire coast, with an incident of 1718 being typical: the discovery of a load of brandy in a Lynn man's home led to a riot, with the smugglers being whipped around the town.

Greenland. A few years later Lynn was sending five whalers each summer to Greenland, leaving in May and returning in July, while the more conventional merchants were trading in wine from Spain, buying lead in Dorset and selling it in France, moving corn to Scotland, buying wood and furs from Norway and Sweden, selling cloth to Denmark, wool to Italy, and doing a small trade in dyes from Picardy.

George Vancouver. It was the perfect background for George Vancouver, born 22 June 1757 in New Conduit Street in a house that no longer exists. As his father was the deputy Collector of Customs at the Customs House on Purfleet, Vancouver had every incentive for a seagoing career, and in 1771 he joined Captain James Cook as junior officer aboard *Resolution* for a four-year voyage around the world.

The year after his return, Vancouver signed on as midshipman on Cook's last voyage, aboard *Discovery*. They failed to find the North-West Passage, but they discovered Hawaii, naming it the Sandwich Islands from John Montagu Sandwich, the corrupt First Lord of the Admiralty. Vancouver was among the sailors who rescued Cook's body after the islanders had murdered him.

Hawaii. Vancouver led his own expedition in 1791, with *Chatham* and *Discovery*, taking Western Australia for the British crown then sailing back to Hawaii where he persuaded the islanders to become part of the British Empire. In return, he presented them with the Union flag, which is still part of the state flag of Hawaii although the British Government never controlled the islands.

Vancouver, B.C. Then he sailed north to Canada, surveyed the west coast in the company of a Spanish captain, and negotiated that a chunk of Canadian territory be ceded from Spain to Britain, eventually becoming British Colombia. Today, the province's largest city is Vancouver, but the man from whom it is named died shortly before his 41st birthday at Petersham, Surrey.

I'd better explain that in 1787 Spanish North America stretched from Central America almost to the Alaska Panhandle, and east to the Mississippi. Vancouver took possesion of Oregon Country which went down almost to Great Salt Lake, and the present US-Canadian border hereabouts was drawn in 1846.

LYNN'S CHURCHES

The oldest surviving church is **All Saints'**, the parish church known to its Saxon founders as All Hallows. All Saints' Day is 1 November, a public holiday in most Catholic countries in Europe, but Britons recognise the day before, All Hallows' Eve, as Hallowe'en.

All Saints' is *not* a Saxon church as much of it was rebuilt in the 14th cent, with few major additions since. The main point of interest is the **anchorhold**, a cell for voluntary prisoners. An anchorite or anchoress, according to gender, was a hermit who asked to be locked into a cell such as this for the remainder of his days as an act of faith. Records show that in 1272, 1477 and the 16th cent there were anchorites in residence here, their human needs fulfilled by a servant living in the next room, who had access to the anchorhold, which had a window and a fireplace. Outside the church on the south wall you can see the scattered remains of the servant's quarters.

St Margaret's. The mother church is St Margaret's, founded in 1101 by Herbert de Losinga, Bishop of Norwich, but you need to be a skilled historical architect to recognise anything of the original. Before the century was out, two moderate towers were added at the west end, guarding the main door; in the 14th cent they were heightened, but soon the north-west tower began to lean as it had been built on poor soil; in 1453 the clergy was obliged to put another tower around it for support, but this time on a larger base. Despite this problem, in the 16th cent the south-west tower had a 258ft (78.6m) spire added. These, plus other modifications, more than doubled the size of the church and made it an encyclopaedic mixture of architectural styles.

Storm. And then came the storm of 8 September 1741 which demolished the south-west tower and its steeple, hurling the masonry onto the nave and reducing much of that to rubble. George III and Sir Robert Walpole, Member of Parliament for Lynn, each gave £1,000, and Parliament allowed the Borough to raise £3,500 by taxation. The tower was replaced, but the steeple was not.

The nave has several treasures, starting with an 18th-cent rack for the town mace when the Mayor comes to church on official business; the Mayor even has his official pew. The richly-decorated pulpit was probably made by Matthew Brettingham, the man who built the main staircase at Holkham Hall; he incorporated the four Hebrew letters of the Tetragrammaton, the name of 'the Unmentionable One,' Jehovah, or Yahweh, reduced (in Latin) to YHWH. Many of the floor tiles were damaged by the flood of January 1978, as was the organ. From 1751 to '60 the organist was Charles Burney who wrote *History of Music* and in 1752 fathered **Fanny Burney,** a popular novelist of the day and author of the memoirs of Madame d'Arblay.

The reredos, an ornamental screen behind the altar, shows Felix, a preacher who was shipwrecked at **Babingley,** near Sandringham, and befriended by badgers when humans rejected him. Felix became the first Bishop of Dunwich, and the inspiration for the name of Felixstowe. And don't miss the side chapel of St John, said to have England's largest brass memorial, to Adam de Walsoken (a village near Wisbech) who died in 1349.

Tides and floods. Medieval King's Lynn has always been subject to flooding, so you won't be surprised by the clock on the outside of the south tower which shows, not the time, but the next high tide, assuming the 'L' to be noon and the 'G' to be midnight. The letters spell the hours as LYNNHIGHTIDE. The tidal clock was installed in 1603, but in the present century the floods have grown worse, as shown by tidemarks at the west door in ascending order: March 1961, March 1949, March 1883, Jan 1953, and the worst to date, Jan 1978. Maybe the sea is rising, but the east coast is certainly sinking.

St Nicholas's Chapel. The town's third church, St Nicholas's Chapel, was built in the 13th and 15th cents and is now used only for concerts during the annual King's Lynn Festival. The chapel suffers from severe subsidence and is not normally open.

Lynn miscellany. Opposite St George's Guildhall are numbers **28, 30** and **32 King St,** hiding the remains of an early medieval stone hall, although from the outside the first two appear half-timbered and the last looks to be 19th-cent. At the Market Lane junction with Chapel St is **Lattice House,** originally a block of shops and homes occupying one long building with thin partitions. Later the building was one of the 400 inns in town, a reminder that until modern times Lynn's water was often undrinkable so beer was the alternative.

Rotten borough. King's Lynn was among the 100 English boroughs granted the right in 1558 to have its own Member of Parliament – but Lynn had *two* members, putting it among the 'rotten boroughs.' At one stage both seats were under the patronage of Thomas Howard, fourth Duke of Norfolk, and the landed gentry competed for the privilege of being elected to such rotten boroughs; in 1675 Robert Coke of Holkham spent £10,000 on his election. The boroughs, of course, expected favours in return, which made them 'rotten.'

Lord George Bentinck, leader of the Protectionist Party, was MP from 1828 to '48 – you'll see the name around town – followed by Lord Stanley, son of the Earl of Derby. The Derby in question was a hamlet on the Isle of Man where the Stanley family lived and where the Eighth Earl of Derby introduced a horse race. Years later the race moved to Epsom and is now world-famous.

Caithness Glass. Not many tourist attractions are in modern factories on industrial estates, but Caithness Glass on the Hardwick Rd Estate is an exception, offering 40-minute guided tours of the glassblowing process Mon-Fri 0930-1600 for £1.20; the shop is open Mon-Fri 0900-1700, Sat 0900-1600, year round. The firm has factories in Oban, Perth and Wick, and moved down to Lynn in recent years, producing a wide range of high-quality glassware, including cut and engraved glass.

Time and tide wait for no man, least of all at St Margaret's Church, King's Lynn.

BEYOND THE TOWN

Before the bypass came, the road to Hunstanton went past Gaywood Clock Tower and **South Wootton,** where the Domesday Book of 1086 mentions the Saxon church. Today's church of St Mary the Virgin probably incorporates part of the Saxon nave, but the remainder is early 14th-cent. A lightning strike brought the tower crashing onto the nave in 1881, which was rebuilt in 1893 with a hammerbeam roof.

CASTLE RISING

Next stop is Castle Rising, which is both a castle and a village. Before the Norman Conquest 'Rysyng' was owned by the manor of Snettisham in the form of Stigand, appointed Archbishop of Canterbury in 1052 and the man who crowned King Harold in 1066. The modern village is small and was rebuilt on its present site in the 12th cent, having been moved to make way for the castle. The church, which has its tower at the transept crossing rather than at the end of the nave, has plaques to several members of the Howard family which produced the Dukes of Norfolk; one is of the second son of Baron Templeton who took the surname after marrying Mary Howard, sole heiress to Richard and the Hon Francis Howard, who had estates here as well as in Staffordshire, Surrey and Westmorland. It seems money was worth more than family, even in those days.

The nearby Babingley River was a tidal creek in early medieval times, hence the rhyme:

Rising was a sea-port town when Lynn was but a marsh.
Now Lynn it is a sea-port town, and Rising fares the worse.

If you know the true Norfolk dialect you can certainly rhyme 'worse' with 'marsh.' You can also rhyme it with 'bus.'

Rotten borough. Castle Rising had its own Member of Parliament – and sometimes two at once – from 1558 until 1832, with Sir Robert Walpole of Houghton Hall among them.

The castle. Rising Castle was begun around 1138 by **William d'Albini,** whose family came from St-Martin d'Aubigny in Normandy, with much of the earthwork done a little later, proved by the discovery of a buried half of a silver penny minted between 1158 and '80 – the coin was cut to make two halfpennies.

Bigod family. William d'Albini was also lord of the manors of Buckenham (south of Wymondham), Happisburgh and Snettisham, and married Maud Bigod, of the family which soon produced the Dukes of Norfolk. He built the priory at Wymondham which became a great abbey in 1449, and where in 1833 workmen found two lead coffins, thought to be of Maud Bigod who died in childbirth, and of her baby. Legend claims that when Maud died her husband gave a silver crucifix containing pieces of the true cross to Wymondham, but this story is remarkably similar to the legend of St Helena who established a monastery in Cyprus (Stavrovouni – it's still there) and gave it an identical cross. Yet another legend claims, wrongly, that Helena was born in Colchester.

Although William and Maud's marriage ended in tragedy, their son, William II d'Albini, married Alice of Louvain, widow of Henry I, and through her gained Arundel Castle in Sussex. Now here's a coincidence: a 16th-cent daughter of the Earl of Arundel, whose tomb is in Framlingham Church, Suffolk, married into the Howard Dukes of Norfolk, mentioned above, which resulted in the Norfolks moving the seat of the earldom to Sussex.

The Albini family continued as earls of Sussex and lords of Arundel, Buckenham and Rising, with William III d'Albini adding to the titles by marrying the widow of Roger de Clare of Clare, Suffolk, whose estates outshone those of the great Bigod family. The fourth William did even better, and was with King John at the signing of Magna Carta, but he died on the way home from the Fifth Crusade in 1221, shortly before the *fifth* William died without heir.

By the mid-13th-cent the castle needed major repairs, which were probably done by Robert Montalt, lord of Rising manor from 1299 to 1329; the King's Bench court records of 1313 also show Robert in dispute over his share of the toll revenue at Lynn and being awarded hefty damages. He sold the castle to newly-crowned Edward III for 10,000 marks (£6,666) in 1327, his widow selling her remaining rights in Rising to Isabella, Edward's queen, in 1331.

Ghost. Edward II was murdered in September 1327, allegedly with a red-hot iron thrust up his anus. His widow, Queen Isabella, imprisoned at Castle Rising on suspicion of being involved in the deed, went mad; the screams of her ghost are said to haunt the castle.

Black Prince. Castle Rising eventually passed to Edward, Prince of Wales and Duke of Cornwall, better known as the Black Prince and son of Edward III. Prince Edward died in 1376, the year before he would have become king, but he had decreed that Rising be passed on in perpetuity to the Duchy of Cornwall; in fact it stayed Duchy property only until 1544, when Henry VIII granted castle and manor to Thomas Howard, third Duke of Norfolk, and his son Henry, the poet **Earl of Surrey**, in exchange for estates around Felixstowe. Henry VIII had Henry Howard beheaded on January 1547 with the duke due to follow on 28 January. But early that day, Henry VIII died and the duke was spared. Now here's *another* coincidence: the tombs of Thomas and Henry Howard are in Framlingham Church with that of the daughter of the Earl of Arundel.

Castle Rising stayed in Howard ownership until 1958 when it passed to the State, and it's now maintained by English Heritage. It's open Tues-Sun year round, 1000-1800 in summer, -1600 in winter, for a small fee; ✆0553.87330.

CASTLE RISING TODAY.

Only the keep and the gatehouse survive, but the keep is impressively large and in reasonable condition, as befits its other name of 'donjon,' from the Latin *dominium*, meaning 'power.' Our word 'dungeon' comes from the same source and has the same meaning, when you think about it. There are ruins of the original Norman church of Rysyng, abandoned when the village was moved, and re-discovered in the 19th cent, but there are only traces of the castle's exterior kitchen, chapel, and lodgings, though the duplicates within the keep are recognisable. The massive earthworks which surround the building are intact, enclosing around 12 acres (5ha), but little remains of the curtain wall that stood on top.

The keep. The keep has distinct similarities with that of Norwich Castle, and both may have been copies of the castle at Falaise, Normandy. The keep is 78.5ft long, plus 20ft for the forebuilding which guards the main door (total 30m), by 68.5ft wide (21m), with walls rising 50ft (15m).

The steps to the main door at first-floor level are impressive, but the great hall, at that same level, lost its grandeur with its floor and roof, leaving a gaping hole 47ft by 23ft (14m by 7m). A booklet available at the castle gives a detailed story and description.

The old Hunstanton road ran through the village, the dangerous bend half a mile north known locally as **Onion Corner** from the smell drifting off the fields. Then, across the Babingley River, you are on the new bypass and entering the Sandringham Estate.

William d'Albini began building Rising Castle, and Edward II's widow is supposed to haunt it.

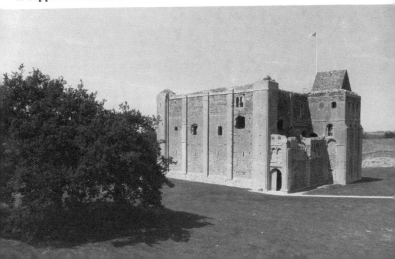

THE SANDRINGHAM ESTATE

Albert-Edward, Prince of Wales, was house-hunting as his parents, Queen Victoria and Prince Albert, wanted him to have a country home of his own when he was 21. On 4 February 1862, Prince Edward saw Sandringham Hall and asked his mother to buy it; Victoria paid £220,000.

The prince added the first of many extensions, and in March 1863 brought his new bride here, Princess Alexandra, daughter of the future monarch of Denmark. More extensions were needed, then still more for the extra staff – then the prince demolished the main part of the house to build from new.

Fire. In November 1891 when the house was empty, fire destroyed 14 upper-storey rooms, but the prince proceeded with his plans to have his 50th birthday party at Sandringham a few days later. The repairs inevitably gave the prince the opportunity to add another suite of bedrooms.

The prince's son, Prince George, Duke of York and later George V, brought his own bride to a small house in the grounds and renamed it York Cottage. As their family was born, so the cottage was extended, and it was here that the future King George VI and all his siblings except Edward VIII were born. The building now serves as the estate office.

Christmas message. The Royal Family tends to use Sandringham House as a winter retreat, and it was from here that George V made his first Christmas Day radio broadcast in 1932, with the Queen giving her first televised Christmas message from here in 1957.

Queen Elizabeth had more major demolition and extensions done between 1973 and '76, concentrating mostly in the courtyard, and in 1977 decided to open the house and grounds to the public.

Opening. Opening times are complex, mainly Apr-Sep, Sun-Thur; House 1100-1645, grounds 1030-1700 (Sun opening 1hr later), but the house is closed around the time of the Sandringham Flower Show in late July, and when any member of the Royal Family is in residence. For latest information, ✆0553.772675 in office hours, or ask at King's Lynn tourist office, ✆0553.761241. Admission: grounds and museum, £2; house, grounds, museum, £2.50 adult. **Sandringham Church** is on the estate and is open at the same times as the grounds, except for local weddings and funerals, plus Oct-Mar Sun-Thur 1100-1230, 1400-1700.

SANDRINGHAM HOUSE

Sandringham House is an elegant country home built of carrstone and brick and splendidly set in gardens of 96 acres (39ha) with mature trees. Visitors can see most of the house interior, including the main two-storey saloon with minstrel gallery, the lady-in-waiting's small drawing room, the main drawing room where family and guests assemble before dinner, the dining room and the ballroom. For a full description, read the excellent coloured guide to the house on sale in the souvenir shop or available from the estate office.

Outside, most visitors' first glimpse of the estate will be the highly-decorative wrought iron **Norwich Gates,** made by Barnards of Norwich for the Great Exhibition of 1862, later a wedding gift for the Prince and Princess of Wales. Inside the gates, accessible along the footpath to the house, is my favourite specimen, the handkerchief tree, which flowers in May.

Museum. The Coach Houses, fire station and estate power house, all to the east of the main house, have been run as the Sandringham Museum since 1973, with the gallery of **Royal cars** being the most popular. Here is a 1900 Daimler Tonneau, the first car bought by royalty and occasionally to be seen in the London to Brighton Rally. Among other cars are a 1913 saloon, a 1928 brougham, and a 1937 shooting brake, all built by Daimler.

Elsewhere in the museum is a fire engine kept for use on the estate, a display of **big game trophies,** and memorabilia of **horse racing** and race horses. Entry is included in the admission fee.

THE ESTATE

Sandringham estate covers 20,104 acres (8,134ha) and includes the villages of Anmer, Babingley, Flitcham, Great Bircham, Shernborne, West Newton, and Wolferton, with a part of Dersingham, and **there is not a public footpath or bridleway anywhere on the grounds.** Sandringham is not a village, although it has a church; in the Domesday record of 1086 it is called *Sant Dersingham,* the first word meaning 'sand.' *Dersingham* may mean 'Deor's village,' hinting at Danish origins.

The estate is the Queen's personal property and is run commercially, its profits helping to maintain Sandringham House. Much of the land is worked by tenant farmers, growing the traditional crops of the area including sugar beet and cereals, but the Queen farms 3,310 acres (1,339ha), has 1,954ac (790ha) under forestry, and 243ac (98ha) devoted to two stud farms. There's also the 117-ac (47ha) fruit farm at Appleton, popular with pick-your-own customers in September and October

THE VILLAGES

The first village after Castle Rising is tiny **Babingley,** whose village sign shows **St Felix** in his ship. Legend claims that Felix built the first Christian church in East Anglia here, around 630, to be followed much later by a stone church abandoned in 1861; the Ordnance Survey map marks the site a mile west of the main road, near the Babingley River and inaccessible. The present church of corrugated iron and thatch near the crossroads was the gift of Edward VII.

From Babingley to Dersingham the soil is almost pure sand, supporting coniferous woods, heathers, and the many rhododendrons that surround Sandringham; it is a beautiful part of the county, particularly in early summer, and is where I, as a child, saw my first grass snake, lizard, and deer. And on Sandringham Warren I found the only sundew – carniverous plants – that I have seen growing wild in Britain.

WOLFERTON Two turnings left take you on a loop road to Wolferton, noted for its railway station, church, and its village sign showing a wolf – but many Norfolk villages boast similar signs, usually showing the origin of the name.

Fenrir and Tyr. This wolf is the legendary Fenrir, an evil beast who terrorised the villagers. The Norse god Woden sent them a slender cord which would restrain Fenrir, if only they could induce him to pit his strength against it. "I will," Fenrir answered, "if one of you puts his right arm in my mouth." Tyr stepped forward to meet the challenge, while others tied the cord around Fenrir's neck. When the beast found he was shackled, he bit off Tyr's hand in his anger, but Tyr considered the sacrifice to be justified. The moral? Never appease evil.

Wolferton Station Museum. The railway runs no more, but the station is popular as a museum, emphasising its connections with royalty travelling to Sandringham. It has kept the Royal retiring rooms built in 1898 for Edward VII and Queen Alexandra, and you can also inspect Queen Victoria's travelling bed, a reconstruction of a Royal carriage of 1890, plus many memorabilia of this particular line. The museum is open Apr-Sep plus Easter, Mon-Fri 1100-1300, 1400-1730, Sun 1300-1700; Sat, craft shop and grounds only; admission around £1.95. ✆0485.540674.

Wolferton Church. St Peter's Church, made from warm carrstone like so many buildings from here to Hunstanton, was built around 1310-'40 near where Felix came ashore to preach the Gospel. Several stone coffins, believed to be 12th or 13th-cent, are on the floor inside the south doorway, probably the same age as the nearby alms box, while the stone seat in the north aisle recalls the days before pews were installed, forcing the aged and infirm to lean on the masonry and so giving rise to the expression that *the weakest go to the wall*.

The south side of the chancel has a small window set low, to allow lepers to follow the service although forbidden to enter.

WEST NEWTON. South of Sandringham House lies West Newton, home to many of the estate staff. East of the village is the water tower built for Appleton Farm in 1877, with accommodation for two small families beneath the tank; this is similar to the 'House in the Clouds' at Thorpeness, Suffolk, where the tank is disguised as a house. South of the village is the derelict church of St Mary, blessed with a round tower but probably Norman, not Saxon; the church was abandoned when Appleton Hall was burned down around 1707 and the Paston family, famous for its letters, moved out.

FLITCHAM. South-east is Flitcham, originally Felixtown and almost certainly another reminder of Bishop Felix. Sir Robert Aiguillan built an Augustinian Priory here in 1251, where Abbey Farm now stands.

ANMER. The road to Anmer climbs one of the steepest hills in Norfolk. The village is tiny, yet was mentioned in Domesday.

GREAT BIRCHAM. Beyond Peddar's Way lies Great Bircham, recorded in Domesday but a site for human habitation since the Bronze Age, as proven by partial excavation of barrows – burial mounds – on the common, which revealed bones and jewellery.

Bircham Mill. The village has a splendid privately-owned windmill, built in 1846 on a site occupied since 1769, and now fully restored, the only working windmill in this part of the county that's open to the public, although there were 300 in Norfolk two centuries ago. You may climb the five floors and see the machinery in motion, and take a privileged look in the mill's revolving cap, this being a tower mill (*Discover the Suffolk Coast* discusses mill types). The tarred brickwork of the tower is 52ft (16m) high, carrying sails 67ft

Never stick your arm down a beast's throat or, like Tyr, you'll have it bitten off. The village sign at Wolferton.

(20.4m) across; the brick bread oven of c1800, with a capacity of 100 loaves, is fired on special days, with its wholemeal produce on sale in the shop.

But that's not all. The mill has a tea room and gift shop (closed Sat), offers occasional pony rides, and **hires cycles** at hourly to weekly rates. Open approx. Apr-May, Sun & Wed; Jun-Sep, daily, 1000-1800, for £2; ✆0485.23393.

War Graves. King George VI unveiled a cross on 14 July 1946 at the War Graves Cemetery by the village church of St Mary the Virgin, where are buried 66 British and Commonwealth air crew, 11 German, and one servicewoman. This is another church to retain its box pews, and its other features include a Norman doorway above which are the Royal Arms of George III before the union with Ireland.

And there's the **Bircham Art Gallery,** where you can choose from contemporary paintings and sculpture or see an exhibition of regional fine art; open Mon-Sat 1100-1730, free; ✆0485.23604.

BIRCHAM NEWTON. The nearby village of Bircham Newton, which is *not* in the Sandringham Estate, is little bigger than Babingley, and its 13th-cent, much-restored church is among the smallest in the county, always ignoring Babingley's example. There are no porches; the south and north doors open straight into the nave. There are no windows on the north wall, only four small ones on the south, plus a small east window. The floor is mostly brick, and the Victorian box-pews are still in place. In short, All Saints' Church would make a good setting for a film on Dickensian poverty.

Yet the church was not poor. In fact, Lord Nelson's daughter Horatia married Philip Ward, the rector of the Birchams, lived for five years at Church Farm, and had a large family. The village was probably of Saxon origin and is recorded in the Domesday Book as Niewtuna, 'new town,' with 'Bircham' added for identification.

R.A.F. Bircham Newton. During World War Two the RAF operated from a large airfield east of the village, rebuilt in 1929 from the Royal Flying Corps base of 1916; 617 Squadron was based here when it experimented with Barnes Wallis's bouncing bomb used in the **Dam Busters** raid. The Air Force moved out in 1960 and in 1967 it became the **Bircham Newton Training Centre** where the construction industry teaches people how to build walls and roofs. The trouble is, somebody else has to knock them down again.

BIRCHAM TOFTS. St Andrew's Church in Bircham Tofts was in use until 1941, although the parish merged with Bircham Newton in 1719, but is now a ruin; its bell, cast in 1705, is in the north aisle of Gt Bircham church.

Tofts? Domesday recorded it as *Stoftstan,* referring to its stony soil. At the Conquest the manor was given to Ode, the Bishop of Bayeaux.

SHERNBORNE. We're back on the Sandringham Estate at Shernborne where the church is on the site of what was probably East Anglia's second-oldest chapel, another indication of Felix's presence; the modern church was rebuilt in 1898 by the Prince of Wales, later Edward VII. The village sign shows St Thomas de Shernborne, who became chamberlain to Margaret of Anjou, queen to Henry VI.

DERSINGHAM. The sea is now 2.5 miles (4km) away at high tide, and twice that distance at low water, but Dersingham was a fishing port in early medieval times, and Henry VI (1422-'61) granted the freedom of the seas to fishermen from the village. On land, Dersingham had seven manors just after the Norman Conquest, including that of Sandringham. The tide has turned, for the Royal Estate now owns much of Dersingham.

St Nicholas's first recorded vicar came in 1106; there's a 12th-cent coffin lid inside the south door; elsewhere there's a wooden chest almost 7ft (2.1m) long, which was known to exist in 1360 – it carries a Latin inscription saying *Jesus of Nazareth, King of Jews*. But the church itself is pure 14th-cent, with Perpendicular windows and hammer-beam roof of the 15th cent.

Great Barn. In the north-west corner of the churchyard stands the Great Barn, now maintained by the county council. It carries the date *1671 July 31*.

Dersingham is also the home of two tourist attractions, provided you ignore the recent bypass and take the picturesque old road. Joan Mullarkey throws porcelain and stoneware by hand at the **Dersingham Pottery** in Chapel Rd, open daily 1000-1750; ☎0485.540761. And Jan and Joe Jackson work the land at **High Farm** with their heavy horses, mainly Suffolk punches, which bring in the crowds Mon-Fri, Easter-Sep, 1230-1700, for around £2.50 which includes demonstrations of how it used to be done, plus rides on the hay wagon, and refreshments in the marquee.

BEYOND THE ROYAL ESTATE

LEZIATE. East of King's Lynn along the B1145 is Leziate, a hamlet which has been carved away to provide sand for building work across the county. The result is some splendid scenery amid the deserted pits, and a good place to find small reptiles on hot summer days. **Gayton** has little to offer as its church is locked and its windmill derelict, but its name is a sharp contrast to that of **Grimston,** to the north. *Grim,* with spelling variants, is the ancient name for the Devil, as in Grimsby (Lincs), the 'Devil's town,' and Grime's Graves in mid-Norfolk, long believed to be the Devil's graveyard until we learned the site holds Neolithic flint mines.

To the south, **East Walton's** church has some box pews, but the ruins of the priory are on private land and therefore inaccessible.

The B1145 leads on towards **Great Massingham,** where St Mary's

Church is locked, but the key is available. The tower is enormous for such a small community. St Andrew's Church in **Little Massingham** was founded by the Saxons, but the oldest part is a solitary Norman window. Sir John L'Estrange was buried here in 1517 because of a clause in his will beginning *If I die within five miles of Massingham...*

HARPLEY. Harpley sits south of the A148, its Church of St Lawrence enlarged between 1294 and 1332, then rebuilt by Sir Robert Knollys (Knowles), commander of the English troops in the wars with France uner Edward III and Richard II. The interior of bare stone and plaster is forbidding, but large. The pews are 15th cent, and the rood probably 14th cent.

Bishops. Earlier churchwardens had a liking for history, as the church has a chronology of bishops of East Anglia:

Felix, 630-647	Thomas 647-653
Boniface 653-669	Bisus 669-673.

Then the diocese was split into two: **Dunwich** in the south, and **Elmham** in the north. The list becomes vague on dates and is far from complete.

North Elmham	**Dunwich**
Bedwinnus (673-9)	Etta (673-)
Northbert	Astwolf
Headulac (-731-)	Eadferth
Edelfrid	Cuthwin
Lanferth	Alberth
Athelwolf (-811-)	Eglaf
Unferth	Herdred
Sibba (-816-)	Alsin
Humferth	Tidferth (787-816)
St Humbert	Weremund
(killed by Danes 870 or 871)	Wibred

HOUGHTON HALL

A mile due north from Harpley is the entrance to Houghton Hall, currently the home of the Marquess of Cholmondeley (pronounced *Chumley*), but built in the early 18th cent for Sir Robert Walpole, the man who created the office of Prime Minister.

The Hall. The hall is around half the size of Sandringham House, externally of strict Palladian design, based on the Italan style of Andrea Palladio, but internally its décor and furnishings outshine those of Sandringham and feature some of the best in the country. Walpole devoted the ground floor to the needs of hunting and other pursuits, while the first floor, reached by grand steps to the main door, was for taste and elegance, pomp and circumstance.

High tide on the coast of Norfolk; Brancaster Creek offers sheltered boating...

The second floor held the guests' bedrooms, including the State Apartment. There are few records of who slept here, but the Duke of Lorraine was a visitor in 1731, sleeping in the Needlework bed; the following year Walpole spent £1,200 on gold lace for the Green Velvet State Bed.

The White Drawing Room is probably the most lavish part of the house, with a richly-decorated high ceiling, gilding on the plaster-work and on the mahogany door, and exquisite furniture by William Kent who also furnished much of Holkham Hall.

Royal Throne. Probably the most astounding treasure inside is the Royal Throne which the Queen uses at the State opening of Parliament and is therefore known to millions of television viewers. Beside it is the throne that Prince Philip sits upon – an inch (3cm) shorter. And beside that are the thrones for the Prince and Princess of Wales.

The stone hall has impressive dimensions, being 40ft (12.2m) in every direction, while the mantelpiece in the parlour is the work of master carver Grinling Gibbons (1648-1720). The house had a splendid collection of paintings, but they were sold to the Empress of Russia in 1779 for £40,000.

Model soldiers. Here is the Cholmondeley Collection of 20,000 model soldiers, claimed to be the most important in the world. See the battle of Culloden Moor of 1746, a skirmish of 1809 in the Peninsular War, the Battle of Isandlwana in the Zulu War, the Battle of Waterloo,

1815, an armoured car attack in the Western Desert in 1942 led by Lt Rocksavage, now Lord Cholmondeley, and many others. The collection was begun at Cholmondeley, Cheshire, in 1928, and moved to Houghton in 1948.

Outside are stables with heavy horses and Shetland ponies, peacocks strolling around the lawns, and a park larger than that of Sandringham House. And this was among the properties the Prince of Wales inspected before deciding on Sandringham.

Houghton Hall is open Apr-Sep Thurs, Sun, bank hols, 1300-1730 (gates close at 1700) for around £3; ☎0485.528569.

Sir Robert Walpole. The man who built Houghton Hall was born on the family estate here in August 1676, the third son and fifth child of parents who had 19 offspring. He was educated at a private school in Great Massingham, then Eton and King's College, Cambridge. While he was alternating between studying the scriptures and sampling the alehouses with friends, his two elder brothers died, leaving Robert heir to the family estates. At the age of 24 he married Catherine, daughter of the Lord Mayor of London, and in November 1701 he claimed his inheritance on his father's death.

Whig. Now controller of the Houghton estates, he followed the family tradition and entered Parliament as the new Member for Castle Rising; his family *owned* the seat. Walpole was, of course, a Whig, and as such he carried the stigma of James I's wrath: *Whiggamor,* the nickname given to the Presbyterians whom James cruelly persecuted, was supposed to resemble the sound made by Scottish peasants as they drove their horses. But then, *Tory* is an anglicised Irish word for the Catholic robbers known as bog trotters.

Moving on to the other family seat of King's Lynn in preference, Walpole rose in Parliamentary prominence through Secretary at War to Treasurer of the Navy, then in 1712 found himself in the Tower of London for having handled £2,000 (some reports say £1,200) in the supply of forage. He was convicted of bribery though he was acting as middleman and never took a penny; in later years he claimed that bribery and corruption were essential elements in the business of statesmanship and that "Every man has his price."

Queen Anne dies. In 1714 Anne was dying of apoplexy and haemorrhage, and the ruling Tory ministers were negotiating the succession of her Catholic step-brother James Edward, when Walpole and other prominent Whigs burst into the royal bedchamber and persuaded Anne to consent to their taking over the administration. This bold strategy allowed the Whigs to proclaim George I as the new sovereign. True, he spoke only German, but at least he was Protestant.

Prime Minister. Walpole continued his career, becoming First Lord of the Treasury and Chancellor of the Exchequer in 1715, thus becoming prime among ministers. From this situation he created the post of Prime Minister – and held it for 22 years, helped occasionally by his brother-in-law Charles, 2nd Viscount Townshend of Raynham Hall, better known as 'Turnip' Townshend. Walpole saved the nation from bankruptcy after the South Sea Bubble scandal, then found himself obliged to offer the new king, George II, an income of £100,000 a year from the Civil List. As the next highest offer was £60,000, Walpole kept his post as Prime Minister – and Townshend retired.

10, Downing St. A grateful George II gave his Prime Minister a town house at 10, Downing St, but Walpole accepted it only as the official residence of the First Lord of the Treasury, which it still is. The Whigs lost influence after a scandal at the Chippenham election, and Walpole resigned in 1742, taking a peerage as the 1st Earl of Orford, with a pension of £4,000 a year. He died on 18 March 1745 in Arlington St, Piccadilly, leaving the Holkham estate deep in debt.

WEST OF KING'S LYNN

Cross the Great Ouse into the Fens and take the A17 almost to the county boundary. At **Terrington St Clement** you will find **Wellbanks Orchid World** and 7,500sq ft (700sq m) of glasshouses full of orchids; ✆0553.827155. Open daily 1100-1700 for £1.50.

Nearby the Rev Tony Clements has run the **African Violet Centre** since 1970, with 3,000 plants to see and buy; ✆0553.828374. Open daily except Christmas week, 1000-1700.

And still in the same village is **Ornamental Conifers and Heathers,** ✆0553.828874, an acre of nursery open Feb-Christmas daily 0900-1700.

...but at low tide the creek is good only for paddling and canoeing.

HUNSTANTON

Pier
Cliff Parade
Northgate
Greevegate
Westgate
OASIS
Seal Island trips
SEALIFE
Park Rd
Southend Rd
KINGDOM of SEA

Traction engine rallies are popular now that these giants have retired from the daily scene.

3: HUNSTANTON

Roman Norfolk

HUNSTANTON CLAIMS THE TITLE of the 'fun resort,' which it achieves while keeping all its charm and character. It is a small town but it can claim several unique features, most important being that it is Britain's only East Coast town that faces west, so you have splendid sunsets over the sea. Look in the right direction at low tide and you may well see 'Boston Stump,' the 272ft (80m) tower of St Botolph's Church, Boston, Lincs.

The resort of Hunstanton was built in Victorian times and owes its existence to the railway but Edward, Prince of Wales, publicised the resort by convalescing here from a near-fatal attack of typhoid. It has a good beach liberally scattered with carrstone boulders, giving plenty of interest for children, and its cliffs north of the stubby pier have white chalk overlaying the red carrstone, a beautiful colour combination.

Hunston, as the locals call it, has little industry and lives for the tourist trade and the many people who have come here to retire. You can see all the town within a day, yet there is plenty to keep families and young children busy all week. Hunstanton has more entertainments than any other Norfolk resort except Great Yarmouth, yet it is still a quiet country town.

Bishop Aelfric of Elmham, who is not listed in Harpley Church, bequeathed land 'acquired under King Canute at Hunstanes tune' to St Edmund's Abbey at Bury; probably this is where the abbots built **St Edmund's Chapel** to commemorate East Anglia's best known saint who is alleged to have come ashore around here; the ruins of the chapel, open daily, are near the lighthouse, which is not open. The saint is also shown in a window of St. Edmund's Church in the *new* town.

Three generations after Aelfric and with the Normans in command, the lord of the manor was Ralph, who held land by courtesy of Roger Bigod, Earl of Norfolk. Ralph's daughter married Roland le Strange who had just come over from Normandy – his family name meant 'stranger' – and for the next 900 years the **L'Estrange** family has lived in Old Hunstanton, latterly at the Hall (not open to the public), a moated mansion severely damaged by fire in 1853. There are tombs for Sir Henry (he died in 1506) and Sir Roger L'Estrange, and a good brass to the latter, in the church of St Mary the Virgin in *Old* Hunstanton, which both men restored. The church also has a Norman font.

Beheaded for theft. St Mary's parish records have the grim evidence in the Assize Roll of 1286, of Nicholas Bagge who was beheaded after a second conviction for theft, believed to be the only known instance of this punishment for larceny in the country.

Entertainments. The new town lost its pier to a storm in 1978, but since then it has added several major attractions. Foremost is **Kingdom of the Sea** on the South Promenade, where you can walk through a plastic tunnel and look at fish swimming above your head. The Kingdom also has a **seal hospital** whose patients are on public view without their chances of return to the wild being jeopardised. The Kingdom is almost a twin of the similar attraction at Great Yarmouth, with both open from 1000 daily except Christmas; ✆0485.533576.

Or is the covered-in **Oasis** the foremost attraction? Whether it's rainy or sunny outside you can enjoy the aquaslide and play squash, as well as battle at table tennis *or* go rollerskating according to season. Opening times are complex; ✆0485.534227 for details.

Adventure excursions. Go take a cruise to **Seal Island,** in reality a sandbank in The Wash, aboard a catamaran for £5 (adult), or experience a ride in a DUKW. The older generation should remember that word is pronounced *duck,* and refers to an American-built amphibian troop-carrier from World War Two. You can even board a Cessna six-seat **seaplane** on the beach and fly off for the day to Skegness. All these excursions leave from the promenade and you can make bookings at the **tourist office** in the town centre, ✆0485.532610.

HEACHAM

You're in for a major surprise when you explore the church of St Mary the Virgin, as it contains a monument to the memory of the native American Princess Pocahontas.

John Rolfe. The Rolfe family had been important in Heacham for generations, and even owned the beach until recent times; and why not, for the L'Estrange family owned the beach at Hunstanton. John Rolfe, born in 1585, sailed for Virginia, America, in 1609, losing his wife and baby in a shipwreck on Bermuda on the way. No matter. Rolfe went alone to Jamestown, the first English colony in North America, founded only two years earlier.

Pocahontas. And there he met and fell in love with Pocahontas, 14-year-old daughter of Chief Powhatan. They married and settled in

Jamestown where Rolfe pioneered the cultivation of tobacco. Their son Thomas was born in Jamestown in 1615, the year before Rolfe sailed home for England, bringing his wife and child.

They certainly came to visit Heacham, and legend claims they planted a mulberry tree in the grounds of the Rolfe ancestral home, Heacham Hall. Then they went to London where Pocahontas was received at the Court of James I.

In 1617 Rolfe and Pocahontas were in Gravesend, preparing to sail back to Virginia, when the princess died. She was buried in St George's Church, but the grave was lost in a later fire. Rolfe sailed on to the New World where he was killed in the massacre of Henrico in 1622.

But why should a native American (we used to call them Red Indians) marry a European? Two years before Rolfe arrived, Captain John Smith (who had worked at King's Lynn) and his party had established the Jamestown colony. Smith had gone exploring, been captured by natives, and taken to their chief, Powhatan, who had decreed that Smith be killed. But the chief's daughter, Pocahontas, had thrown herself between Smith and the executioner and so saved his life. She became the link between the Amerinds and the Europeans, and was the first native American to be baptised, when she added the name Rebecka (Rebecca) to her own.

The story ends with the Pocahontas memorial in the church, installed in 1933; the destruction by fire of Heacham Hall, the Rolfe

The growing coastline: sand dunes planted with marram grass on the western coast of Norfolk...

family home, in 1941; and the death of the last of the Rolfes in 1990.

The church. This story began in the church, so let's return there. The proposed 'chapel' was mentioned in 1248, and the architecture is certainly of that time. The tower is at the central crossing, and needed an enormous buttress in 1802 to prevent its collapse. The single bell was cast in the early 12th cent and believed to be the oldest in East Anglia. And the brass chandeliers were from the Rolfe family, copies of those in St Mark's Basilica, Venice.

Organised labour. Heacham takes a place in the history of trades unionism as it was on 5 November 1795 that 110 poor farmers and 106 day labourers met in the church to organise their labour and so claim a reasonable wage – 39 years before the Tolpuddle Martyrs had the same idea. The Heacham attempt failed because the Government introduced its Anti-sedition Laws that same month, following an incident at the State opening of Parliament in which the crowd threw mud and stones at William IV's carriage.

Is it just coincidence that **Moss Evans,** the former leader of the Transport and General Workers' Union, moved to Heacham in 1987 and was elected district councillor for the village in 1991?

NORFOLK LAVENDER.

Roughly opposite the church is Caley Mill, home of England's only commercial lavender farm. Founded by Linnaeus Chilvers in 1932,

...and the eroding coast; a stretch of cliffs near Sheringham that is under threat from the sea.

Norfolk Lavender now has around 100 acres (40ha) on which it grows five types for harvesting, but it is building up a 'living dictionary' of every variety – can you add to it?

The Romans perfumed their bath water with lavender, and the plant's name comes from the Latin *lavare*, 'to wash.' The Tudors used lavender and charcoal to clean their teeth, added it to beeswax for polish, and perfumed their tobacco with it. Later it was added to soap, and Norfolk Lavender supplies oil distilled on the premises to Yardleys, the perfumiers.

The company is Britain's sole distiller of lavender oil, producing half a ton in a good year – but French lavender farmers around Grasse squeeze 1,000 tons a year.

Norfolk Lavender's grounds are open all year, free, with guided tours Spring Bank Hol-Sep; the gift shop is open daily (excl Xmas) 1000-1700; the conservatory shop, for lavender and other plants, Easter-Sep 1000-1700; and the tea room daily 1030-1700. Coach trips to more distant fields June-Aug, Mon & Fri; ✆0485.70384.

The beach. Heacham has beaches to north and south of the village. The sand is good for building castles but at low water mark a mile offshore, it becomes muddy. Caravan sites dominate the coastline inland of the narrow creek which is all that remains of the medieval Heacham Harbour; boats no longer use it as there is no navigable access to the sea. Beyond the creek is a large car park with fee.

SNETTISHAM

Snettisham is the village that has the quarry that yields the carrstone that's used throughout the district. But it has three tourist attractions as well, starting with Park Farm.

PARK FARM. This is a genuine working farm signposted to the eastern fringe of the village where on 329 acres you and the children can witness the lambing season in March and April, the deer calving in June and July, and all other farming activities during the opening season, Apr-Oct, daily (possibly not Sat) 1030-1700; you can also take a safari ride through the deer park. Venison and free range eggs are available in the shop.

Three signposted trails lead visitors around the farmyard or further afield, and there are play areas for the children, a craft shop, tea shop in converted farm buildings – and picnicking in the orchard. ✆0485.42425.

Church. The nearby church of St Mary has a splendid spire but is normally locked, an indication of visitors of the wrong kind.

WATER MILL. The long road down to the shore passes Snettisham Water Mill, *erected in a time of scarcity by public subscription for the benefit of the neighbourhood, 1800*, according to a sign on the front wall. Restored to working order, the mill once again grinds wheat for flour Easter, late May-early Sep, Wed & Thur, 1000-1730; admission for adults £1 – and the mill shop sells the flour. Show the children the Lego exhibition, the ducks on the millpond, and the small waterfall.

SNETTISHAM COASTAL PARK. At the end of the long road is Snettisham Coastal Park, an important wildlife refuge run by the district council. Stretching 1.8 miles (3km) north to the first caravan on Heacham south beach, the 143-acre (58-ha) park is an important wildlife habitat and was created to remove further human pressure on the fragile environment. The warden is usually on duty by the main entrance at the Snettisham end Apr-Sep daily 1400-1600, but the park is always open, with lavatories near the entrance and an observation hide half-way up the coast at the end of a signed 'blue trail.' The warden lives at Village Farm, Ingoldisthorpe, ✆0485.41239.

Keen birdwatchers can expect to see many of these species, according to season (**R** = resident, **PM** = passage migrant, **SM** = summer migrant, **WM** = winter migrant):

Bunting, reed, R	Partridge, R
Coot, R	Pheasant, R
Curlew, R	Pintail, WM
Dunlin, R	Pipit, meadow, R
Flycatcher, spotted, PM	Plover, R
Goldfinch, R	Redpoll, R
Goose, brent, WM	Redshank, spotted, PM
– pink-footed, WM	Redstart, PM
Greenshank, PM	Sanderling, WM
Harrier, marsh, R	Sandpiper, common, PM
Heron, R	Scoter, WM
Kingfisher species, RK	Skylark, R
Knot, WM	Snipe, R
Lapwing, WM	Swallow, SM
Linnet, R	Swan species, R
Mallard, SM	Swift, SM
Martin, sand, SM	Teal, R
Merganser, WM	Tit, bearded, R
Moorhen, R	Turnstone, WM
Ousel, ring, PM	Warbler species, SM
Owl, short-eared, R	Whitethroat, SM
Oystercatcher, R	Wigeon, R

Lepidoptera. In habitat ranging from scrub to reed to open water, several species of butterfly and moth are found, including: Burnet, Gatekeeper, Grayling, Green-veined white, Large hawk, Meadow brown, Orange tip, Peacock, Small copper, and Tortoiseshell, small and large.

Flora. The flora is mainly salt-tolerant, including sea purslane, sea holly, sea lavender, sea campion and sea poppy, with some glasswort, better known in this area as samphire.

The beach. Snettisham beach has good sand at high water mark, but low water exposes more than two miles of sand with a growing amount of mud. There is no proper beach south of the village as the mudflats of the Great Ouse estuary are too close for comfort. This is a splendid area for exploring, but you **must be properly equipped** as there is a risk of being cut off by the incoming tide, with fatal results.

Rose and Crown. Back in the village, the Rose and Crown is a 14th-cent coaching inn on Old Church Road that has plenty of character; ✆0485.541382.

Snettisham treasure. Snettisham's fourth tourist attraction is in the British Museum; it is a gold bracelet of around 70BC which is part of the Snettisham treasure. There is evidence that man has been living in this area from Neolithic (new stone age) times.

INGOLDISTHORPE. The village of Inglesthorpe, which is how you should prounce its name, has nothing to attract the visitor beyond its charm; even its church is redundant and locked.

THE NORTH COAST

East from Old Hunstanton the first village is **Holme next the Sea,** a tiny, pleasant village north of the main road. It has a wide **beach** of fine sand, with pools at low water; access is mostly on foot across the golf links, and there are no services to spoil the beauty of nature – pack your gear in, and pack your rubbish out.

Church. The 15th-cent church of St Mary has a tower 76ft (23m) tall, almost separated from the nave which has an austere interior. It was built by Henry Notingham (with one 't') who was a judge to Henry IV (1399-1413), but it was always too big for the village. In 1778 much of the ruined nave and both aisles were demolished, resulting in today's bizarre ground plan. Notingham's brass is the main feature of interest, with this inscription:

Henry Notingham & hys wyffe lyne here
yat maden this chirche stepull & quere [choir]
two vestments & belles they made also
christ hem save therefore ffro wo
and to bring her saules to blis of heaven
sayth pater & ave with mylde steven.

There is no longer a 'stepull' (steeple), and the Notinghams' graves are outside as the church vanished from above them; no trace remains, although there are plenty of headstones for the Nelson family, distant relations of Lord Nelson.

Napoleon. Now here's a coincidence. Ann Jane le Clerc of this parish had a daughter who became Mrs Matthew Nelson. But Ann Jane was niece of General le Clerc, uncle by marriage to Napoleon Bonaparte.

Peddars Way. The village is the northern terminal of Peddars Way, the Roman road from Colchester to Lincoln via a ferry across the mouth of The Wash to around Burgh le Marsh (Lincs). Nothing remains of the road south of Knettishall Heath, near Thetford, but from there to Holme it is in good condition although with many minor diversions.

Where the Peddars Way stops, the Norfolk Coast Path begins, meandering to Cromer; together, both paths total 86 miles (138km) and received Department of the Environment approval in October 1982, with Prince Charles officially opening them in July 1986.

Holme Bird Observatory. The village has a bird observatory run by the Norfolk Ornithologists' Association with the Norfolk Naturalists' Trust reserve and nature trail nearby: see chapter 1.

THORNHAM

Boadicea (Boudicca), queen of the Iceni tribe of East Anglia, destroyed the Roman city of Colchester in 62 in retribution for Roman treachery. The Roman govenor Paullinus counter-attacked and triumphed, killing 80,000 Britons for the loss of 400 Romans, and with Boadicea killing herself by poison.

After that, the Romans began their colonisation of East Anglia, improved the roads, and established several settlements and forts along the north Norfolk coast.

They built one such fort at Thornham, its ruins being discovered in 1948 by a study of aerial photos, although a few small artefacts found earlier in the area are in the Castle Museum, Norwich. Excavations at the fort revealed a Saxon cemetery with 22 skeletons, all of which went to Norwich.

Church. The Saxons began building All Saints' Church – their south porch and priest's room above it, remain – but most of the present building postdates the Black Death of 1348-'50 which killed 800,000 Britons. By 1845 the nave roof had collapsed and the bell was in the churchyard, but over the next 50 years the repairs were done.

Bats. After World War Two, when a large colony of bats had moved into the church, the vicar and congregation went on the attack by draping a net across the door and killing hundreds of bats with tennis rackets. Thankfully, attitudes have changed since then.

But back to the Black Death. A clump of trees west of Staithe Lane, leading to the harbour, marks the site of Thornham's mass grave for its many victims.

Mill. A windmill and a separate watermill were on Staithe Lane in the 13th cent; both have gone, but a 1:12 scale model of the windmill is in the church.

The dissolution of the monasteries in 1536-'7 resulted in Henry VIII seizing much Church property, including Thornham Manor, which he gave to his physician William Butts, co-founder of the **Royal College of Surgeons.** A later lord of the manor, George Hogge, began Thornham Hall in 1788, its south-eastern entry today marked by a whale's rib for a gatepost.

Ironworks. The last of the Hogge line, a girl, married into the Ames Lyde family and gave the name, and the village, considerable fame by starting a wrought-iron foundry in 1887. It was probably a passing idea, but the ironworks succeeded, though always with family subsidy. By 1894 it had a staff of two, but five years later 25 men were working full-time producing, among many other items, the kitchen garden gates for **Sandringham House** and decorations for Balmoral Castle. Royal patronage was the key to greater success, and soon orders were coming from the Empire. In 1900 the smiths made three gates for the Royal Pavilion at the Paris Exhibition, perhaps their greatest achievement, but the business collapsed in 1914 with Mrs Ames Lyde's death and the outbreak of war. The smithy closed in 1920 and is now the Thornham Service Station.

Local art and craft. Sidney Maher runs **Craft Collection** from London House, on the south side of the main road; ✆0485.26221, Easter-Xmas. The collection offers a wide range of craft souvenirs, including pottery and glassware, jams and spices, woodwork and basketry, wool, leather, embroidery and jewellery – plus lavender toiletries and wrought iron. Brian Day runs the **Studio Gallery** from his home, selling his own high quality watercolours, and prints from them as greetings cards.

Lifeboat Inn. The late 16th-cent Lifeboat Inn was a working farmhouse for generations, and qualified to become an alehouse as it had a window opening onto the road – a strange ruling. Its name comes from the introduction of the lifeboat at Hunstanton. As smuggling was rife, the village had Customs men in lodgings on several occasions, some of them inevitably staying at the inn.

Beach. The beach is difficult to reach along a mile of the Norfolk Coastal Path, and is therefore uncrowded, but the sands are excellent.

TITCHWELL. Titchwell has its RSPB reserve (see chapter 1) and, beyond it, an equally good beach. The church has a round tower but using stone probably from Normandy for the windows – so is it a Norman tower in Saxon style or a Saxon tower with Norman additions? Nobody knows.

BRANCASTER and SCOLT HEAD ISLAND

Little is visible of the Roman fort at Branodunum, and it was not until 1960 that the remains of the Romano-British cemetery and Christian

Sheringham Beach: the groynes help check erosion of the sand.

burials of the 4th cent were discovered near the church.

The beautiful village of Brancaster, whose name may perhaps mean 'burned castle,' knows nothing of its Roman origins and survives today for tourism and shell-fishing. The 14th-cent Church of St Mary the Virgin, a successor to the building that King Edgar the Peaceful of Mercia (959-'975) gave to Ramsey Abbey, has an elaborately-carved font cover 7ft (2.1m) tall, which telescopes when raised for christenings. Elsewhere a plaque recalls the village's **lifeboats** *Joseph and Mary* (1874-'93) which saved 28 people, the *Alfred S Gerith* (1893-1919) which saved six in three launchings, and the final boat on this station, the *Winlaton,* which never saved anybody.

BRANCASTER STAITHE. The hamlet of Brancaster Staithe, now larger than Brancaster itself, developed as Scolt Head Island grew, and flourished in the 18th and 19th cents. In 1797 it had a malt house, claimed to be the largest in England at the time, but the building was demolished in 1878. Sailing ships imported coal and exported grain and malt, but today the harbour is devoted almost entirely to pleasure craft. You can launch your own boat, or hire one.

Mussels are still farmed in the harbour, transplanted here for three years from spawning grounds in The Wash, and whelks are dredged from the sea bed 15 miles (24km) away.

Beach. A good road leads to Brancaster beach, with a pay car park available, owned by the nearby Royal West Norfolk Golf Club. The sand is good and remarkably clean, and you could find remains of an ancient forest that was drowned as the North Sea rose at the end of the Ice Ages.

National Trust. The National Trust, which owns almost everything between the Norfolk Coast Path and low water mark, from Brancaster to Burnham Harbour, including most of Scolt Head, has an **information centre** at Brancaster Staithe, open late Mar-late Jul Sat-Sun 1000-1800, late Jul–Aug daily, same times; ℭ0485.210719. You can also **hire cycles** on daily or weekly rates, and rent self-catering accommodation, for which contact the warden.

Scolt Head Island. Scolt Head is an island around 3.7 miles (6km) long, which continually changes its shape and has been growing throughout recorded history. Its northern coast is a series of sand dunes protecting the salt marsh on its southern shore. It is uninhabited and little-visited, which is fortunate since the island and its wildlife are very fragile.

The National Trust bought Scolt Head from Lord Leicester of Holkham Hall in 1923, with the Norfolk Naturalist Trust buying the eastern tip in 1945; the Nature Conservancy Council leased the entire island for 99 years in 1953.

Scolt Head has England's largest breeding colony of Sandwich terns, and other breeding species include the little, the Arctic and the common tern; ringed plover and oystercatcher; black-headed gull, redshank and greenshank; gannet, kittiwake and Arctic skua. A marked trail assures minimum disturbance of the bird residents, with the ternery closed to visitors in May and June.

Access by boat is from Brancaster Staithe each morning, times depending upon weather and tide. Dogs are not allowed Apr-Aug.

Samphire. The salt marshes around Brancaster, Wootton near Lynn, and indeed in all suitable locations on the east coast, grow large areas of samphire, an edible seaweed that is on sale from King's Lynn to Cromer in high summer. Samphire, pronounced *sam-fur*, is a corruption of the French name, *l'herbe de Saint Pierre*, known to botanists as glasswort. It looks like strings of tiny green sausages in the form of a Christmas tree, up to 6in (15cm) tall, found around the high-tide mark.

To prepare it, wash thoroughly, cut off the roots, then steam or boil until the flesh is tender. For ease of eating, hold the plant by its base, put it in your mouth and pull it out, your teeth scraping off the flesh; the polite way is to do that on the plate with a fork. Samphire must be eaten within a day of harvesting as it cannot be preserved satisfactorily, even by pickling.

INLAND FROM HUNSTANTON

DOCKING. The largest inland village for miles was originally called Dry Docking as it is on a hilltop almost 300ft (90m) above sea level, with no permanent stream nearer than Fring. The villagers dug a well in 1760, and at 237ft (72.2m) they struck water, which was then sold at a farthing (0.6p) a bucket. In 1928 a pump was installed, which had to work without breaking a law of physics that states that if a column of water is lifted more than 32ft (9.75m), it collapses. Not surprisingly, the supply was interrupted occasionally, and in 1934 people were buying it from Bircham Newton airfield at a ha'penny (1.2p) a bucket.

Church. The oldest part of the Church of St Mary the Virgin is the chancel, built before the Black Death of 1349-'50, but there are hints that an earlier church had connections with Aelfric, Bishop of Elmham in 1038. The 80-ft (24m) tower was under construction when Henry V, despite defeating the French at Agincourt in 1415, grew suspicious of all French-owned religious houses in England. As a Norman order owned Docking Rectory, Henry seized it and kept it in the Royal family until Henry VI gave it to Eton College.

The church's greatest treasure is its 15th-cent font, with bas-relief statues of 14 saints, all beheaded – the statues, not the saints – at the Reformation of 1552.

STANHOE. The village of Stanhoe is tiny, but its 14th-cent Church of All Saints has a wall tablet remembering Sir William Hoste of Burnham Market who fought in the Battle of Lissa (Croatia, 1866). But why was an English captain involved in a war between Italy and Austria?

Other villages. Poor **Fring's** only claim to fame is that it was mentioned in Domesday – but so was **Sedgeford,** where the Saxon church's round tower has survived, entombed in the later masonry of the present square tower. **Ringstead** breaks conventions by having a *Norman* round tower to its St Peter's Church – but the church was abandoned in 1771 and now only the tower survives, in the grounds of the former rectory. But that was Ringstead *Magna*, and there was also a Ringstead *Parva*, otherwise known as Barret Ringstead, whose church, St Andrew's, was abandoned in the 19th cent and has disappeared.

So now there is just Ringstead and its own distinctive Church of St Andrew.

Views. The road from Ringstead to Holme, and the lanes south of Thornham, offer splendid views across The Wash and on a clear day you can see the Lincolnshire Wolds.

4: WELLS-NEXT-THE-SEA

Nelson's Norfolk

WELLS MADE MUCH OF ITS LIVING in medieval times from plundering shipwrecks. As the definition of a wreck was a vessel on which no living creature had survived, those men first at the scene often had some unpleasant business to conduct. Wells men in particular developed the nickname of *bite-fingers* from their time-saving method of removing rings from corpses.

Although it is 'next-the-sea' and not 'on-sea' (it keeps the hyphens while Holme next the sea does not), Wells has lived on maritime trade from its beginnings until this century. The earliest mention of Wells was in the 13th cent, and in 1404 37 of the ships visiting the port were seized by pirates from Dunkirk.

The north Norfolk ports, including Blakeney and Cley, could manage vessels up to 160 tons, which was larger than any of Columbus's ships: *Santa Maria* weighed 90 tons and the *Pinta* and *Niña* each weighed 60.

Harbour Commissioners. An Act of Parliament in 1675 created the Wells Harbour Commissioners, who could then charge 6d (2.5p) for every tun or last handled. A tun was 252 gallons (1,145 litres) if wine, less if beer; a last was 640 gallons (2,909 litres) of grain or other dry goods. This was a heavy tax for the time. In 1770 and 1835 other Acts were passed, the latter changing the duty to a shilling (5p) per *ton* (not 'tun') of the ship's registered tonnage, which still applies today.

Lifeboat. An Act of 1844 allowed the commissioners to buy property around the waterfront and build the present quay, which meant the demolition of around 28 cottages and sheds. The Act also ruled that a lifeboat be provided, with a £2 a day fine if it were not seaworthy; this rule continued until the Royal National Lifeboat Institute installed its own boat in 1869.

Sea wall. Back in 1758 one Sir John Turner began draining the marshes inland towards Warham, but in 1858-'59 the Admiralty gave permission to Lord Leicester of Holkham Hall to build a sea wall due north from the town, cutting off 588 acres (2.37sq km) of marsh as well as the tidal access to Holkham village, which had been a minor port for centuries. Soon after, Wells harbour began silting, probably because the embankment was dead straight, and the only straight line that nature allows is the horizon.

Silting never became a major problem, and so Wells harbour continued trading, becoming prosperous from around 1850 to 1914 although suffering a drop in business when the railway came in 1857. Cargoes were mainly coal in and malt and barley out, with Guinness long being a major buyer of the malt. Trade changed after 1918, with potash a new import and sugar beet a growing export.

Whelks. The Second World War stopped almost all activity as Wells became an Air-Sea Rescue base. Whelk fishing recovered quickly, with Wells soon supplying around 60% of the nation's needs, but general trade was in the doldrums with 14 ships a year. Favor Parker bought the quayside in the early 1970s and increased the import of animal fodder, but export business was still slack.

The trend continues, with variations. For example, in 1985 248 shiploads were imported, totalling almost 100,000 tons – but 9 shiploads were exported, at 4,150 tons. And since then trade has declined: 1986, 218 shiploads in, and the last one to go out; 1987, 207 in; 1988 151 in, bringing 75,000 tons of cargo; 1989 down to 121 in; and 1990 just 51 shiploads in, carrying 19,268 tons.

The problems with Wells are twofold: there is a draft limit of 10ft (3m), available only on spring tides matching new and full moons – and dredging is totally uneconomic. Wells will never rival Felixstowe.

Pleasure craft. As commercial shipping declines, so the private sector grows, with a variety of yachts at permanent moorings in the outflow creek. Boats capable of more than 15 knots (28kph) are allowed in the harbour only for access to shore, and all boats must obey the 5mph (8kph) speed limit. Jet skiing is prohibited in the harbour, and windsurfing there without a permit can bring you a £100 fine.

Further down the outfall creek, jet skiing, windsurfing and swimming are allowed in strictly separated areas. The **channel is narrow and fast-flowing,** so weak swimmers must be careful.

As Wells has the only commercial harbour between King's Lynn and Great Yarmouth, it is popular with private yachtsmen on passage, and offers 700ft (200m) of quay mooring, plus chandlery, water, fuel, pilotage, and a slipway. Harbourmaster: 16 High St, ✆0328.711744.

Disasters. On Tuesday 27 February 1898 the naval gunboat *Alarm* heaved-to (stopped) at sea and launched its shoreboat. But the weather was treacherous and the shoreboat overturned, drowning six of its crew. The coastguard boat put to sea to help, capsized, and drowned five more men. Eleven men therefore died in an exercise which was merely to deliver a copper lamp to the harbourmaster's office! Favor Parker's silo on the quay has marks showing the flood levels reached on 11 January 1978 (16ft 1in, 4.91m) and on 31 January

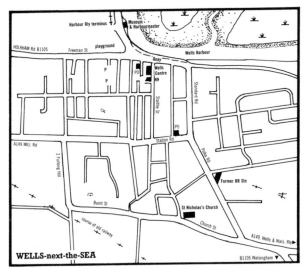

WELLS-next-the-SEA

1953, the day of the Great East Coast Flood (16ft 10in, 5.13m) when the Heacham-Wells railway was destroyed at Holkham and a small ship was lifted onto the quay at Wells.

Museum. Wells Museum, which opened on 27 July 1991 at the back of the Harbourmaster's office (Sat, Sun, Wed, 50p), has photos of the stranded ship, and many other aspects of Wells's history, including a model lifeboat, radio equipment from a fishing vessel, aspects of Lord Nelson, and the story of fishing and wildfowling in the area.

Wildfowling. Wells was probably the best place in the country for wildfowling in the early 20th cent; this was a popular pastime for the aristocracy who took up to 15,000 pink-footed geese and 5,000 white-fronted geese in a season – but it was an essential source of food for the working class.

Tide measure. Near the museum is a strange box on a pillar, with steps leading up to it. This is the National Rivers Authority's tide measure, which relays information by phone, in Morse code.

Harbour Railway. Wells has two 10.25in-gauge (26cm) railways, both owned by the same man. The Harbour Railway runs the length of the straight sea wall built in 1858, from the museum to the coastguard lookout and the lifeboat station by the beach; there's also a good pay car park here. Trains operate Spring Bank Hol-Sep with up to 18 return trips daily from 1030-2300 for 45p single, serving Pinewood Caravan Park and camping sites.

Beach. The beach, beyond the sea wall, is splendid, with large dunes above high-water mark, held in place by marram grass planted by the Coke family of Holkham Hall. The beach has absolutely no services – but in this designated **Area of Outstanding Natural Beauty,** that's how it should be. By the way, the AONB follows the coast from Hunstanton to Mundesley, and then from Sea Palling to Winterton-on-Sea.

WELLS and WALSINGHAM RAILWAY

The other 10.25in-gauge track is the Wells & Walsingham Light Railway which ran its first service in March 1982 along the route of the Wells & Fakenham Railway which closed in 1964.

British Rail took up its track and sold the land, so the WWLR had to start almost at the beginning, even to removing 3,000 tons of rubbish from a cutting at Walsingham and spreading the remainder, giving a gradient of 1-in-29, among the steepest in Britain and a problem that British Rail never had. The private enterprise line started with one locomotive, *Pilgrim*, an 0-6-0 side tank engine with two 6in by 4in cylinders working to 125psi (8 bar), custom-built by David King of North Walsham. The loco had to haul four coaches carrying 42 passengers up that 1-in-29 grade.

The trouble was, the WWLR was too successful, attracting not only tourists but local people as well, and in peak season the train could carry only half its intending passengers.

Rolling stock. A fifth carriage was added in 1985, giving a payload

The Wells and Walsingham Railway claims to have the world's smallest-gauge public service railroad – 10.25 inches.

of 52, but also taking poor *Pilgrim* to its limits. Later that season *Weasel*, an 0-6-0 powered by a 1300cc Ford petrol engine and built by Alan Keef of Bampton, Oxford, was added to stock as a reserve. Meanwhile, the owner ordered another custom-built steam loco, the *Norfolk Hero*, consisting of two 2-6-0 locos mounted back-to-back and sharing a fuel box and driver's cab. It has four 6in by 4in cylinders generating 140psi (9 bar), measures 20.39ft (6.21m) long by 34in (0.864m) wide, and can take a curve as tight as 75ft (23m) radius.

Timetable. The WWLR, claiming to have the smallest gauge of any public railway in the world, operates on four miles (6.4km) of track which it covers in 25 minutes. Season: Easter-Sep, daily; low and high season timetables with up to six return journeys 1000-1720, plus evening excursion and driving lessons. No phone number.

The old station in Wells now holds **Burnham Pottery** (open Mon-Sat 1000-1700, ✆0328.710847) while the new station, in the restored signal-box, has a gift shop. The old station in Walsingham is now a church.

St Nicholas's Church. Wells's patron saint is Nicholas, who cares for children, fishermen, merchants, travellers, pawnbrokers and a few others, and who was the original Santa Claus. Nicholas gave three bags of gold to finance a merchant's daughters' marriages – hence the three gold balls as the pawnbrokers' symbol.

The first church on this site was probably built around 1229, the first known vicar was appointed in 1302, and the place was rebuilt around 1460. Then on 3 August 1879 lightning struck the tower and the church was gutted in the resultant fire. St Nicholas's was rebuilt by 1883 to the same design and using much of the original masonry, but at a cost of £7,000.

Two objects of interest escaped the fire: the brass eagle-style lectern was buried in a field until discovered by a man with a pick (see the hole in the lectern) – but nobody knows if the eagle was buried to hide it from Cromwell's men, or whether it was they who threw it away. The other survivor was the church chest, bearing the carved date 1635 as well as scorch marks said to show that the chest was dragged from the fire just in time.

The parish register records the baptism of John Fryer, sailing master of HMS *Bounty* on Captain Bligh's ill-fated mission. Fryer's headstone was moved and his grave cannot now be identified.

Playland. Wells caters for a fair range of holidaymaker: dinghy sailors, windsurfers, water skiers, nature lovers, walkers and cyclists. Playland, near the quay, is purely for the children, open daily in season 1000-1730; ✆0328.711656.

Tourist Office. The tourist office is in Staithe St near the quay, Apr-Oct, hours vary, ✆0328.710885.

HOLKHAM HALL

Let's begin with Robert Coke, born in Mileham, 6 miles (9.5km) south of Fakenham, but a lawyer at Lincoln's Inn, London. His son Edward, born 1550, studied at Norwich and Trinity College in Cambridge. Called to the Bar, he later married Bridget Paston, heiress to that family fortune, and built Godwick Hall (q.v.). He also led the trial of Sir Walter Raleigh and Guy Fawkes, but that's another story. With a few kinks, the family tree branched out to Thomas Coke who did the Grand Tour of Europe before conceiving in 1718 the idea of building an elegant home on the family estates in Norfolk. Eleven years passed before the work began, and that was only an obelisk.

Now let's jump to the Earldom of Leicester, a title created soon after the Norman Conquest and held by Simon de Montfort, among others. Several familes qualified for the earldom, and it eventually passed to Thomas Coke who, by then, had planted the great avenue of beeches on the Holkham estate. In time the estate would grow to 3,200 acres (5 square miles exact, 12,95sq km) and be part-surrounded by a brick wall 9 miles (14.5km) long.

Thomas died in 1759 and his countess followed in 1766, leaving Holkham Hall to her great-nephew **Thomas William Coke,** born 1754. But the title didn't go with the estate; indeed, it passed to the **Townshend** family from 1784 to 1837 (see Houghton Hall), but that's yet another story.

Thomas William Coke, Earl of Leicester, became Member of

The majestic front of Holkham Hall.

Parliament in 1776, the year he inherited Holkham, and stayed there with few interruptions until 1833. In 1837 he inherited the title from the Townshends and became Earl of Leicester, and in June 1842 he died; he's buried in Tittleshall (q.v.).

Thomas William, better known as Coke of Holkham, was an important character, the man who popularised the 'Norfolk system' of farming in which crops were rotated on a four-year programme: wheat; turnips; barley, with clover sown at the same time; the clover on its own, for grazing. This simple plan replaced the three-year lay – wheat or rye; barley or oats; fallow – and revolutionised farming by allowing livestock to be fed overwinter instead of being slaughtered in the autumn. The extra dung increased fertility of the soil, and so increased crop yields.

Turnip Townshend. Yet Coke couldn't have done it alone. Charles Townshend, the second Viscount Townshend of Raynham Hall, 5 miles (8km) south-west of Fakenham, had studied the cultivation of turnips and clover in the Netherlands, and so made Coke his raw materials. Charles was brother-in-law of Robert Walpole, Britain's first Prime Minister, but he is better known in history as 'Turnip' Townshend. His grandson Charles, as Chancellor of the Exchequer, imposed taxes on the New England colonists and so prompted the Boston Tea Party and the American War of Independence, but that's yet another story.

Jethro Tull. Both men owed part of their success to Jethro Tull, born in 1741, the man who invented the horse-drawn seed drill and so abolished the practise of broadcasting it by hand. Seeds sown in straight lines were easier to weed, and could be hoed by horse-power, another factor to increase yields.

The ideas of all three men flourished because the feudal strip-cultivation system was being being abolished in favour of a man owning a set piece of land outright, with the incentive to plan his crops and improve the soil. Parliament had already approved the change by passing the Enclosures Act, which brought major changes to the English countryside: hedges separated the new, smaller fields, and cottages went up on the new farmsteads. Half the farmland had been enclosed by 1750, and the results of the combined efforts of the pioneers are apparent in statistics. In 1700 England produced 13,000,000 quarters of wheat, but in 1820 the yield was 25,000,000 quarters.

A quarter? That's an old method of measuring bulk, not weight, and equalled 64 Imperial gallons.

Building the Hall. But what of Holkham Hall? Building of the main house began in 1734 and was to take 27 years, William Kent designing Holkham as well as Houghton. Kent saw it as a giant H, the vertical strokes – the hall's double fronts – each 344ft (105m) long and rivalling

A part of the Bygones Collection at Holkham Hall – but there are more traction engines to be seen at the Thursford Collection.

the enlarged Sandringham House for spectacle. The style was pure Palladian and had to include all the treasures that Thomas Coke had brought back from his Grand Tour.

Thomas William Coke made full use of the hall, entertaining up to 700 guests at a time to the annual Holkham Shearings, which were in effect Britain's first agricultural shows.

The interior. It is difficult to decide which is the more impressive, the lavish building or its sumptuous contents, which include many works by Gainsborough, Rubens, Van Dyck, and others. The alabaster entrance hall is a masterpiece which sets the tone of what is to follow as you walk through room after room, seeing exquisite furniture, much of it made by William Kent, and enormous tapestries hanging on the walls. At one time Holkham's library grew to such such size and importance that many books had to be moved to the Bodleian Library at Oxford, and the collection is now one of Britain's biggest, exceeding the impressive one at Blickling Hall.

The gardens. When Thomas Coke died, his widow the countess commssioned Lancelot 'Capability' Brown to design the ornamental gardens. It was so fashionable for the aristocracy to engage Brown that when he died in 1783, aged 68, he had made a great fortune. However, the grounds at Holkham show that Brown had great skill as well.

The Garden Centre. Today the 6-acre (2.5ha) walled kitchen garden, still holding the orangery and vinery, grows roses, alpines, bedding plants and house plants for sale; it is **open** year round, Mon-Sat 1000-1700, Sun 1400-1700; ✆1328.710374.

Holkham Pottery. The estate opened Holkham Pottery in 1951 to make high quality souvenirs, and you can see the potters and painters at work Mon-Fri 1400-1630; ✆0328.710424.

Bygones: The vast collection of old household items that featured on Anglia Television's *Bygones* programmes is now permanently housed in Holkham's converted stables. You can find steam engines and fire engines, motor bikes and milk churns, a smithy and a laundry, and much else besides. Other attractions include a gift shop (Easter-Oct), an exhibition of the History of Farming, and a cruise on the park's lake aboard the present Lord Coke's electrically-powered launch.

Open. Holkham Hall is open Sun-Thur late May-Sep, 1330-1700; bank hols Sun-Mon 1130-1700. Adult's admission to park plus Hall *or* Bygones is £2.70; to everywhere, £4.70; ✆0328.710227.

Holkham Church. Holkham village clusters around the start of the long drive up to the hall, but the village church, dedicated to St Withburga, is a mile to the west and inside the encircling wall. It stands on a mound built by the Saxons, hinting that a Saxon chapel was here. The plaques inside indicate that this is very much a memorial to past members of the Coke family.

THE BURNHAMS and LORD NELSON

There are six villages in the Burnham group: Burnham Market, the main village a little above the tiny River Burn; Burnham Overy Staithe, where yachts can still moor – *staithe* is a Norfolk word for 'quay' – Burnham Overy Town, which is scarcely big enough to be called a hamlet; Burnham Deepdale, which is no bigger, and snuggles up beside Brancaster Staithe; Burnham Norton, which was the 'north town' of the group; and Burnham Thorpe, birthplace of one of England's greatest naval officers, Admiral Horatio Nelson. Older Ordnance Survey maps marked Burnham Westgate, Burnham Sutton and Burnham Ulph in addition.

Nelson. Edmund Nelson was a curate at Beccles in 1744 when he met Catherine Suckling, a great-niece of Sir Robert Walpole. Edmund went on to become vicar of Hilborough, near Swaffham, but returned to Beccles to marry Catherine in his old church. The Nelsons moved to Downham Market and had had three or four of their 11 children before the Rev Edmund was appointed rector of **Burnham Thorpe** in 1755. The sixth child was Horatio, born 29 September 1758 in a house called the Shooting Box as the rectory was being redecorated; he was seven weeks premature and was baptised within hours as nobody expected him to live, then he was baptised again, properly, on 6 October 1758.

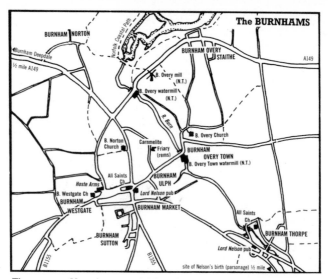

The young Horatio started his education at the Royal Grammar School in Norwich then at 11 moved to the Paston Grammar School in North Walsham, probably because Frances Paston, descendant of the school's founder, was friendly with Catherine Nelson; their bodies lie only a few feet apart in Burnham Thorpe church. Mrs Nelson died when Horatio was nine and, at the age of 12, the lad heard that his uncle, Maurice Suckling, had been appointed captain of the 60-gun *Raisonnable*. Nelson begged his father's permission to join the Navy as a 'captain's servant.'

Nelson's early naval career took him to the West Indies, the Arctic, the East Indies and the Mediterranean, seldom returning to Norfolk. He was commander of the *Boreas* when he met Frances 'Fanny' Nisbet, niece of the President of the Council of Nevis, in the West Indies; they were married in Nevis in 1787.

Lady Hamilton. Nelson came home soon after and, bitter about Naval orders, opted for half-pay and spent the next five years at Burnham Thorpe, occasionally visiting the Walpole estate (William Pitt was then Prime Minister) and Thomas William Coke's estate at Holkham. At last he was appointed captain of the *Agamemnon* in 1793, bound for the Mediterranean where he met Lady Hamilton at the Court of Naples; the two were to become surreptitious lovers.

Eye and arm. Nelson lost his right eye in 1794 off Corsica and his right arm in 1797 off Teneriffe, but he was now a national hero, a Knight of the Order of the Bath and Rear Admiral of the Blue – at the

The Annunciation Altar in the Holy House at Little Walsingham and (below) the impressive church in the tiny weaving village of Worstead.

Norfolk Lavender near Hunstanton has Britain's only commercial lavender farm. The Benedictine Order moved into Binham Priory around 1091.

Cley Mill, one of the most popular subjects for artists and photo-graphers.

age of 38. He came home to Burnham Thorpe where Fanny nursed him for seven months, then he went off to the Battle of the Nile, a victory which brought him the title of Baron Nelson of the Nile and Burnham Thorpe. His final battle was off Cape Trafalgar on 21 October 1805, where he was killed. His body was landed at Rosia Bay, Gibraltar, and shipped home to England in a barrel of brandy. Nelson had hoped to be buried at Burnham Thorpe beside his parents, but instead his remains lie in the crypt of St Paul's Cathedral, in a sarcophagus originally intended for Cardinal Wolsey, the Ipswich lad who rose to prominence.

The Government gave Nelson's two surviving sisters £1,000 each; his elder brother received an earldom, an income of £6,000 a year, and £100,000 to buy an estate; Lady Nelson received a pension of £2,000 a year; Lady Hamilton received nothing and died destitute in 1815. And the nation received Nelson's Column in a major London square that was renamed from a remote Spanish headland: Trafalgar.

The _Lord Nelson_ pub. The only pub in Burnham Thorpe is aptly called the _Lord Nelson,_ which was in advanced decay when Les Winter took it over in 1966. He has restored it as near as possible to its condition when Nelson held his celebration party here before joining the _Agamemnon,_ and made it a museum to the admiral. Having researched the Nelson saga Winter concludes that the admiral's private life was in such a mess – Emma had borne him an illegitimate son – that Nelson dressed in his finery and stood prominent on the deck of HMS *Victory* at Trafalgar, hoping that death would bring a solution. Indeed, his final words to one of his own captains before the battle were: "God bless you, Blackwood. I shall never see you again."

The village of Burnham Thorpe was in the Holkham Estate around Nelson's time, but Holkham has retreated, its western boundary now being along a Roman road that seems to go nowhere.

All Saints' Church. The exterior of the east wall of the parish church has a chequerboard finish identical to that of the Trinity Guildhall in King's Lynn, built in 1421. A similar design is on the heraldic shield of Sir William Calthorpe in All Saints' chancel floor and, as he died in 1420, church authorities assume Sir William was responsible for the east wall. The Calthorpes also left their mark in the churches at Anmer, East Barsham and Cockthorpe.

Entrance is through the north porch, with the crest of HMS *Nelson,* a ship of World War Two, fixed on a nearby wall; her flag is in the north aisle with that of HMS *Indomitable* of World War One. Among the concessions to Lord Nelson is a pre-1801 (the year of the union with Ireland) Naval Ensign which flies from the tower on suitable days. The rood was a gift from Canada in Nelson's honour while the cross above it, and the lectern, were made from wood from the *Victory.* The great chest was made from panels from the Rev Edmund Nelson's pulpit, and the hassocks show *Victory* under full sail. Finally, a bust of Lord Nelson adorns the chancel wall.

THE VILLAGES

BURNHAM DEEPDALE. Tiny Burnham Deepdale, three miles from Burnham Market, has a Saxon round tower of c1040 on its church of St Mary, although later restoration is suspected. The single bell was cast in King's Lynn in the 14th cent.

The Norman font was damaged during major restoration in 1797, and spent the next 40 years in the garden of Fincham rectory, near Downham Market. The restored font shows 12 panels of the farming year seen from the labourer's point of view.

Local artists sell their work through the **Anchor Gallery** on the main road, open daily Mar-Dec 1000-1700; call in for a selection of water colours, pastels, oils or acrylics of Norfolk land- and sea-scapes.

BURNHAM NORTON. St Margaret's Church at Burnham Norton has a round tower – so is it Saxon? Some historians believe the recesses of the windows suggest Norman stone mouldings, which would make it a post-Conquest structure: a Saxon tower built in Norman times, probably around 1090. The nave and chancel were rebuilt in Early English and Perpendicular style, taking them into the 15th cent, and the impression today is that the church interior would make a wonderful setting for a medieval film, except for the modern pews.

St Margaret's has several other unusual features. For a start, there's a bread oven on the west side of the north porch, presumably used for baking Communion wafers; the hexagonal Jacobean wineglass-shaped pulpit is claimed to be the best in England; for most of its life the church has had two rectors jointly appointed, making this a 'mediety;' and the church is a mile from the village.

Mediety. The last point is simple to explain: the village grew up around the church but moved, probably during the Black Death of 1346. The mediety is difficult to understand, but the nearby villages of **Burnham Ulph** and **Burnham Sutton** (west and south of Burnham Market respectively), shared the one church and rector, the parish being known as Sutton-cum-Ulph. The name is easy: Ulf was a Dane who owned the manor, and Sutton is the opposite of Norton. In 1952 the parishes of Norton, Westgate, Sutton, and Ulph were united, and since 1969 they have been held in plurality – a modern version of mediety – with Thorpe and Overy.

Burnham Norton Friary. Due east of Norton's church but down a side lane, stand the remains of the Carmelite Friary, the home of the white friars, who took their name from Mount Carmel in modern Haifa, Israel, captured by the Turks in 1238; Sir William Calthorpe of Burnham Thorpe was one of two co-founders in 1241.

The friars thrived, extending their property in 1249 and 1353, and a record of 1505 shows that a Thomas Giggles left them 6/8d (33p) in his will.

At the dissolution of the monasteries in 1538, the friary owned 68 acres (27.5ha) but the four remaining inmates were too poor to maintain the buildings. Lady Anne Calthorpe wanted to buy the place but the Vicar-General Thomas Cromwell, Earl of Essex (not to be confused with Oliver Cromwell the dictator), refused until he had stripped out the lead, the bells, and the silverware – then he sold it to her. It passed to the Pepys family, relatives of the diarist Samuel, then to the Walpoles, and finally to the Coke family. Today it is an insignificant ruin opposite the school.

The simple difference between a friar and a monk? The former travelled to preach; the latter stayed in one place.

BURNHAM WESTGATE. Burnham Westgate's church of St Mary the Virgin has a tower built around 1310, and in the north aisle a window in memory of Sir William Boulton who helped Nelson on several occasions.

BURNHAM OVERY. At Burnham Overy we see another example of a village uprooting itself. The community was originally around St Clement's church in Burnham Overy Town, but the problem here was that the River Burn gradually silted: in medieval times, seagoing vessels moored just below the watermill, due east of the ruined friary, but when this was no longer possible the community moved to Burnham Overy Staithe, leaving the church behind. St Clement's was a Norman structure with the tower at the centre, an experiment which seldom succeeded as the base of the tower lacked strength; today the tower arches are bricked in, giving the impression of two naves sharing a common tower.

You can take boat trips from Overy Staithe to **Scolt Head Island** from Bill Haines's marina.

Mills. There are *three* mills in Burnham Overy: a privately-owned watermill strides the Burn on the B1155; and the National Trust owns the other watermill downstream, on the A149 a mile downstream, where the complex of buildings, dating from the late 18th cent, includes a malting floor. The last is a windmill 100m to the east, built in 1816 and restored in 1986 for £26,000. None of the mills is open to the public, the National Trust properties having tenants installed.

The Hoste Arms. Sir William Hoste, born in the Burnhams (some authorities say Ingoldisthorpe) in 1780, served under Nelson in several campaigns, but missed Trafalgar. The Hoste Arms is a 17th-cent hotel-restaurant in Burnham Market, the oldest hotel in the area and built for people coming to the local assizes (courts). The inn was a staging post on the coaching run between Lynn and Norwich, and was probably where Nelson collected his weekly newspaper during his years 'on the beach' before joining the *Agamemnon*.

The CREAKES

Burn is a word of Germanic origin, meaning 'small river.' *Creek* is a word of similar origin with the same meaning. The River Burn flows through Burnham – 'settlement by the river' – yet it's not known as the River Creake where it passes the twin villages of the Creakes.

The B1355 south from Burnham Market passes close to the ruins of **Creake Abbey,** an Augustinian community founded by Sir Robert de Narford and his wife in 1206. In 1504 all the priests died of the plague in one week and the abbey ceased to operate. It's now owned by English Heritage and is permanently open, free.

NORTH CREAKE. The church of St Mary the Virgin is probably 12th-cent, and the dedication is specifically to the *birth* of Mary, while St Mary's church at South Creake concentrates on her *assumption* (arrival in Heaven). The nave is large and high, with an impressive hammerbeam roof and an ornate rood screen, with traces of the rood stairs visible. Several surviving wills mention work on the tower, with Nicholas Aleyn leaving £20 in 1435, Margaret Jeye leaving 26/8d (£1.33p) in 1450, and Margaret Forster adding 10/– (50p) for the bells in 1470 – but none of the bells predates 1744.

Yet another Sir William Calthorpe is shown in a large brass, probably of 1505, holding a model of the church which he rebuilt.

Sir Edward Coke's impressive memorial in Tittleshall Church recalls the man who built Godwick Hall. His relations did far better: they built Holkham Hall.

The Rev Thomas Keppell, rector from 1844 to 1863, served under Capt. Frederick Marryat who retired to Langham and turned to writing novels, notably *Masterman Ready* (1841) in which Keppel was the model for the character of Mr Midshipman Easy.

Forge Museum. The old village forge in Church Street has kept up with the times by *not* keeping up with the times, and so opening its doors to a living museum of the blacksmith's art. In this rambling flint smithy you can see the old-style charcoal forge fired by bellows, and examine some of the tools that were made in places such as this in great-grandfather's time. The tea rooms offer blacksmiths' lunches, and the River Burn runs through the tea gardens. Open weekends and school holidays in summer, 1200-1700; ✆0328.738910.

SOUTH CREAKE. St Mary's at South Creake is a similar church, with a good rood screen, and an ancient locked chest. At the south end of the village, **Country Crafts and Gallery** mounts a permanent exhibition of paintings by local artists, and sells local crafts. Open 1000-1700; ✆0328.823563.

EAST FROM WELLS

WARHAM. The Burnhams have prepared us for more churches than there are villages, but Warham went to the extreme and had *three* churches, all at the same time. **St Mary Magdalene** is the main one, amid the lime trees in the village – you can easily drive past the gateway. **All Saints** is a towerless church by the crossroads to the east, and locked; and **St Mary the Virgin** was to the west of the village, but only the foundations remain. In addition, there are records which mention a chapel.

St Mary Magdalene has traces of Norman work in an arch on the north wall, but building continued into the 15th cent. If you appreciate medieval architecture, look at the priest's door to the chancel, set in a λ-shaped buttress. The interior is strikingly simple, with the old box pews still in place.

The English language. The list of priests is almost complete from 1278 to the present. Every one until 1377 has a name with the French *de*, 'of,' in it, then comes Andrew Goldsmith whose surname is of Germanic origin: it would be *Goldschmied* in modern German and *goudsmid* in Dutch. This echoes the origins of the English language itself, with the Saxon-speaking people suddenly overrun in 1066 by French speakers. From then on the language in the manor hall was French; *mouton*, *boeuf* and *poule* for the mutton, beef and poultry at table, while the servant classes who tended the animals still spoke a Germanic language; *Schaf, Ochs* and *Hühner* in modern German for the sheep, ox and hen they tended, but seldom ate. Only when plague, famine, and the end of serfdom eased the social barriers, did the two languages unite to form English, a speech with German grammar and a predominantly French vocabulary.

By the way, that list of priests includes Thomas Robert Keppell whom we saw as North Creake's priest 1844-'63. He was in charge of the combined parish of Warham St Mary Magdalene and St Mary the Virgin from 1837 – but records don't mention another priest until 1874: could that be an oversight?

The chapel is a testimony to the **Turner** family who settled in Lynn around 1670. Charles Turner paid for the Exchange, now the Customs House; the Duke's Head inn on Tuesday Market for merchants using the Exchange; and the Market Cross. This Charles married Mary Walpole, sister of Prime Minister Sir Robert, and Charles's brother John became one of the two MPs for Lynn in 1712-'13, in effect 'keeping the seat warm' for its regular member, the future Prime Minister, while Walpole served his time in the Tower of London. When Walpole was released, John Turner resigned from Parliament and Walpole regained the seat – and if you don't believe this, read the Latin inscription on John's tomb.

Nepotism. If you want an example of nepotism, consider that there were times when *both* Lynn seats in Parliament were held by Turners.

The Turners bought the Warham estate in 1709, but in 1604 it had been the property of Thomas Howard, the Earl of Surrey who was beheaded that year. The earl's tomb in Framlingham Church, Suffolk, is claimed to be the most heavily-gilded in *Europe* and is worth a 100-

mile diversion.

The last of the Turners died in 1780, and five years later the celebrated Thomas Coke of Holkham bought the estate and demolished the house. His last words are claimed to be on his two regrets in life: the demolition, and allowing hay-making on a Sunday.

Warham Camp. Turn south at the crossroads by All Saints' Church, climb the hill, and look for a tiny "footpath" sign at the crest. A cart track leads west to the vast double-ring earthwork of Warham Camp, covering several acres and with mounds 30ft (10m) high. **Iron Age** relics were found here in 1959, plus a Saxon midden (rubbish tip). It's on private land but you can visit it at any time.

STIFFKEY. Everybody seems to know that Stiffkey is pronounced 'Stewky,' yet the people who live there pronounce it as it is spelt. Truth is, *Stewky* was the spelling in the 16th cent.

It is a charming little village, at one time dominated by Stiffkey Hall, south of the little river, which the Bacon family began in 1578. At its prime around 1650 the hall had 80 rooms, but most of it was destroyed by fire in the 18th cent; remains include the west wing and a gatehouse dated 1604.

Two churches. The village had a church in 1066 – but which one? Records show that St Mary's was built in 1310 and a second church, St John the Baptist's, was added in the 15th cent, each with its own rector. St Mary's was demolished in 1558 – you can see a trace of it in the churchyard – and St John's was extended, its nave made wider and the building converted into a smart example of the Perpendicular period. But which church stands on that original site?

The surviving St John's uses red brick mixed with the white flints which are found in this part of the county; flint is usually jet black inside.

COCKTHORPE. South of Stiffkey is the tiny village of Cockthorpe. The church of St Andrew and All Saints is redundant, but maintained by the Norfolk Churches Trust; the key is at the farmhouse opposite. The church is built of rubble and the walls were originally plastered, a mix showing that funds were scarce. Inside it is equally plain and simple, as if unaltered for centuries, and there's another tomb to a member of the Calthorpe family, this time Sir James who died in 1615. His wife, who was born Barbara Bacon, is remembered with him in a wall plaque which explains:

> *By her he had 8 sons and 6 daughters, in whose several marriages and issues the ancient glory of the name and family...did reflourish and is dilated into many of the best houses in the county.*

And when Barbara died at the age of 86 she had 193 descendants.

Cloudisley Shovell. Two English admirals were baptised here, which outstrips Burnham Thorpe: Sir John Narborough, who served under Blakeney man Sir Christopher Myngs in the second and third Battles of North Foreland, 1 June and 25-6 July, 1666. The other man was Sir Cloudisley Shovell, who also sailed under Myngs as well as under Narborough. He helped in the capture of Gibraltar in 1704, but his ship, the *Association*, was wrecked in the Scillies in 1707. Around 1737 a dying woman confessed that Shovell was washed ashore alive, but she killed him for the emerald ring on his finger.

COCKTHORPE HALL TOY MUSEUM.

Cloudisley Shovell was reputedly born at Cockthorpe Hall, a 16th-cent house in brick and flint that is now the home of the Cockthorpe Hall Toy Museum, open daily, mid Feb-Oct, 1000-1730; Mon-Fri rest of year 1100-1600, £2. As Christmas, toys and children go together, the museum features Santa Claus in Toyland at various dates from late Nov; ✆0328.830293 for more details and separate admission fee.

David Kidd and his family began collecting toys in the early 1970s, and the museum is the result, holding thousands of playthings, the great majority made in the 20th cent. Here are model railways from the Hornby gauge '0' (1.25in, 31.75mm) to 3.5in gauge; Meccano sets; tinplate lorries, cars and aircraft following the tradition started in Nuremberg; diecast lead soldiers made by Taylor & Barratt, Britain and others; Teddy bears and dolls from 1920, and dolls' houses from the Victorian era to 1960, including the four-storey 'Gordon House' of c1870; and toys powered by battery, electricity, clockwork, or even just a rubber band.

There are games and puzzles, including a selection made by the now-defunct Hobbies company of East Dereham; and there are toys for adults – a Sinclair C5 electric car, a polyphon, a phonograph, and magic lanterns. Athanasius Kircher, a Jesuit priest, invented the magic lantern around 1640 and accidentally scared his audiences into thinking he was a sorcerer. And there's a tea-room.

LANGHAM. On the opposite side of the wartime Cockfield airfield is Langham, a small village that was known as Langham Episcopi after Pope Alexander III gave it to the Bishop of Elmham in 1176. Most of the present church is 15th Cent, on 14th cent foundations; it was originally dedicated to St Mary in 1603 but after a bishop of Norwich (the diocese was created when Elmham was divided) wrote that it was *whollie ruynatd and p'faned long since* ('wholly ruined and profaned') restoration began and St Andrew was added to the patron St Mary. Two of the three bells were cast at Blakeney in 1699 and 1702, a strange place to find a bell-foundry.

The novelist **Captain Marryat** lived in the village 1843-'48, and was lost at sea on 20 December 1848.

The Augustinian Canons built the priory at Weybourne, but they moved out before Henry VIII demolished the country's religious houses.

LANGHAM GLASS

North of the village centre, the flint Long Barn built in 1722 has been converted to hold Langham Glass, a workshop where high-quality lead-crystal glassware is blown and shaped in the traditional way, with limited use of moulds. Master glassmaker Paul Miller and designer Ronald Stennet-Wilson started the business here in 1979 with the aim of producing the finest quality possible.

Visitors are able to watch the process from a viewing gallery as the soft glass comes from the furnace at 1,100°C and passes from one craftsman to the next as each blends his skills. Langham glass is now exported worldwide, but you can buy from a selection of items in the shop, with decorative paperweights, colourful animals, and artistic wine glasses the favoured designs. There's a children's play area and tea room.

The shop is open Mon-Fri, New Year-Xmas, 0900-1700, plus Sun and bank hols May-Sep; ✆0328.830511; admission £2 allows a discount on purchases.

MORSTON. On the coast is the small village of Morston whose inhabitants firmly believed in the Second Coming. The church of All Saints, built in the 13th cent and enlarged later, received a lightning strike to its tower in 1743, demolishing the masonry. As the villagers believed Christ was due to make a return visit quite soon, they saw no need to repair the tower. Only when they realised that Christ wasn't keeping the appointment did they do the repair.

Inside, look for the carving on the first corbel on the left after the south door, which shows the village gossip with his or her tongue hanging out. You'll probably also notice that the church is noticeable poorer than the trio at Blakeney, Wiveton and Cley, where there was much better access to the sea in the Middle Ages.

Morston Quay. A lane leads to Morston Quay where you have a choice of boat to take you out to see the seals on the sandbanks, some of which are becoming permanent islands; there's also the chance of a visit to **Blakeney Point,** depending on the season, the tide, and the weather. Departures vary from 0930 to 1830, dictated by the times of high tide, sometimes with two sailings in a day. Fares are £3 for adults, £2 for children; contact John Bean at 12 The Street, ✆0263.740038, *or* Temple's Ferry at the Anchor pub, ✆0263.740791 or 0328.830420.

BLAKENEY and BLAKENEY POINT

The Domesday record of 1086 refers to *Esnuterle* and *Snuterlea,* a name which may mean anywhere on a bleak location; from this root Middle English evolved the verb *sniteren,* 'to snow,' and its associated noun *snitter,* a 'bitter wind,' both of which can apply to Blakeney in midwinter. But where is – or was – the village of Snitterley? There has been no coastal erosion here since the retreat of the glaciers, yet nobody has found any trace of a possible community on an exposed hill or headland.

The name *Blakeneye,* probably meaning 'black island,' appeared in 1230, inferring it was a separate community, but in the 14th and 15th cents the village of Blakeney was known by both names. *Every* place-name in East Anglia which ends in *-ey* or *-ea,* shows its Norse or Danish origins, as this was their word for 'island' – but don't confuse it with *-lea,* which meant 'meadow,' or *-leigh* which has other origins.

Finally, 'Snitterley' was used when referring to the manor, the church or the friary, and 'Blakeney' when talking of the harbour and its trade. My theory is that the village was built on the exposed 'bleak coast' but found shelter when the 'black island,' now Blakeney Point, gradually encroached from the east. Why black? Some people suggest it was named from Blekinge in south Sweden; why not?

Busy port. The fact remains that Snitterley-Blakeney was a busy port in early medieval times, sending grain, and salt from the evaporating pans at **Salthouse** – which explains that village's name – in return for fish. Henry III granted Snitterley a market in 1223, and in 1326 Blakeney was listed as one of the country's 59 ports permitted to trade in horses, money, and precious metals: a trade which required the presence of a merchant who had sworn an oath to the king.

Edward III controlled the sale of fish at Snitterley in 1358, as there was a big fair or market at Blakeney; after this, the name of Blakeney seems to have taken precedence.

St Nicholas. The size of St Nicholas's church (open daily to dusk) infers that the community, by whatever name, was prosperous, even though churches in East Anglia are frequently large enough to hold twice the present population of the parish. In Blakeney's case the nave probably served the village while the chancel served a **Carmelite Friary** established in 1296 and completed in 1321. The friary was north of the windmill – which is not a tourist attraction – on the site now occupied by Friary Farm.

Very little is known of this friary, but St Nicholas's chancel has a brass plaque bearing a Latin inscription in Gothic characters which, translated into English, reads:

𝕳ere lie the bodies of 𝕵ohn 𝕮althorp, knight, one of the founders (a mistake: it should read 'benefactors') of the convent of friars, and of 𝕬lice his wife, who died the 16th day of 𝕬ugust 𝕬𝕯 1508, on whose souls may 𝕲od have mercy.

Sir John's will, drawn up in 1503, states that his *Synfull body* was *to be beryed in the White ffryes of Sniterlie, that is to say in the myddys of the chancell,* and that's roughly where the tomb is, on the north side of the chancel. Sir John died 22 August 1503, his widow surviving him by almost five years.

The best-known associate of the friary was Sir John de Bacons-thorpe, born 1290, educated at the friary, and later known to practice medicine in Paris. One record claims he died in 1316, another that he returned to England in 1329. In view of the discrepancy, it's not your fault you've never heard of him.

Two towers. The church nave was rebuilt around 1435, making it distinctive from the original architecture of the chancel. At the same time the great west tower was added, 104ft (31.7m) tall according to the church guide but 120ft (36.5m) according to other sources. One bell survives, cast in 1699. But the strange thing about St Nicholas's church is its *eastern* tower, probably built around the time of the friary. Nobody knows its purpose, some suggesting it was a primitive lighthouse for navigators, visible 20 miles (32km) out to sea; some claim it was a belltower. Others argue that the taller tower would have been far better as a light (but what happened before it was built?), and that the east tower was not strong enough to survive the vibrations of a medieval bell tolling.

Mappa Mundi. Records of 1368 show that the church had a *Mappa Mundi* which might have been something like the famous World Map in Hereford Cathedral, although historical sceptics doubt it. It's gone, so there's no way of knowing.

Parish records and registers were recorded in fair detail from 1538, but the most interesting marginal notes come from 1727-'81, when Henry Calthorpe was rector. He noted the 'Great Snow' of five hours on 3 May 1698; the brief storm of 25 October 1772 when hailstones in Blakeney were '4in in girth' (10cm) but no other villages had any at all; and the sturgeon 7ft (2.1m) long caught in Blakeney Pit, the channel north of Morston.

Census. A census taken in 1580 had reported the population of Blakeney as 360, with the village owning 12 ships of tonnage ranging from 16 to 100; Wiveton had 13 ships, the smallest being of 40 tons; and Cley, with 450 people, had 9 ships for fishing the waters off Iceland, the smallest a mere 20-ton vessel, the largest 100 tons.

Spanish Armada. The Mayor and Aldermen of Lynn, acting on orders from the Privy Council – the council for the Crown – requested the villages of Blakeney, Wiveton and Cley, collectively to provide a vessel or supplies to be sent against the approaching Spanish Armada in 1588. One version has Lynn reporting back to the Privy Council that the trio *were not willing to be at any charge near the furnishing of a ship,* the act of defiance not so much anti-patriotic as a protest at suspected extortion from Lynn. Another story claims that all the seamen were away, fishing off Iceland, while a third story states that Blakeney and Cley contributed to the Royal fleet. There are several such discrepancies and contradictions in the story of Blakeney...or is it Snitterley?

We can be reasonably sure that the seamen of the three villages enjoyed an enviable reputation in high places; the fishermen were long exempt from the Press Gangs which would snatch men off the

Blickling Hall is so big that it's nice to take a break and stretch out on the lawns.

streets and from the fields for immediate recruitment into the army or navy on an unlimited engagement. Many pressed men never even had the chance to see their families again.

By the early 16th cent the Dutchman Van Hasedunck had been commissioned to reclaim the marshes at **Salthouse,** which prompted Sir Henry Calthorpe to build a causeway between Blakeney and Cley and so cut the port of Wiveton from its access to the sea. After strong local protest the Privy Council ordered the bank to be demolished, but it was too late to save Wiveton harbour from silting. The 17th cent saw sweated labour building the vast shingle bank from Salthouse towards the sands of Blakeney Point, so enclosing the harbour for evermore, and in 1823 the Calthorpes built further sea walls to claim more saltmarsh. The two operations greatly reduced the volume of water which surged into the Glaven with each tide, and so caused silting at Cley and Blakeney, and ultimately the destruction of the villages' commercial traffic, although Blakeney continued shipping coal and grain until World War One.

The Guildhall. Blakeney's so-called Guildhall is a 14th-cent building close to the harbour but difficult to find: look behind the flint building with a clock on its gable. The main feature of the place is the cellar (the undercroft), where you have an early example of bricks being used to build a vaulted ceiling. This may be all that remains of a merchant's house – or was it part of the friary? – but it's unlikely ever to have been a Guildhall, and that's *another* ambiguity. English Heritage owns it, and it's open at any time with no fee.

The quayside Blakeney Hotel, opened in 1923, replaced the Crown and Anchor pub, which the locals used to call the Barking Dickey. The Manor Hotel began life prosaically as the manor house, and the White Hart Hotel rents out cycles as a sideline.

Lifeboat. The Norfolk Association for Saving the Lives of Ship-wrecked Mariners introduced a simple oar-driven lifeboat around 1820, based on Blakeney Point for a speedy response, though there were sometimes delays in getting crewmen out to the point; around 1860 eight men drowned when they were answering a call in their own boat. The RNLI took over in 1861 but closed the station in 1925.

BLAKENEY POINT

A group of people bought 407 acres (164ha) of Cley Marshes in 1926 and days later founded the **Norfolk Naturalists' Trust,** England's first county-based conservation body. The National Trust had owned part of Blakeney Point since 1912, and now owns all the 'tween-tides mudflats south of the headland, and most of the salt marshes at Morton and Stiffkey as well. Access is by boat from Morston, or on foot from Cley along the narrow gravel bank.

The peninsula is forever changing its shape as tides work on the shingle bank that faces the open sea, and winds play with the loose sand at the western end, where the main tern-nesting area is. At least 256 species of bird have been seen on the point, with 11 nesting species, including common, little and sandwich tern, ringed plover, oystercatcher, and other waders, while species such as the bluethroat, wryneck, avocet, bearded tit, bittern and Lapland bunting are seen most years. The point is also a major feeding-place for spring and autumn migrants.

The colony of common seals which has been here for years was reduced from around 700 to 200 by the mysterious epidemic of 1988, but numbers are now increasing.

Blakeney Point claims an impressive list of flora as well, with more than 190 species of flowering plants recorded.

The old lifeboat house has survived the ages, and is now a refreshment hut April-Sep, while nearby is a lavatory for ♿ visitors, who can travel in their wheelchairs along a 400ft (120m) boardwalk – but *the warden must be forewarned of a disabled visitor* on ✆0263.740480 Apr-Sep, 0328.830401 Oct-Mar. **Dogs** must be kept on a lead at all times, and are not allowed near the ternery Apr-Aug.

Blakeney Point Sailing School. The Blakeney Point Sailing School which opened in 1991 has no connection with the point beyond its name. It offers instruction on small boats from the simple Mirror dinghy to a racing catamaran, with much of the tuition being done in Blakeney Harbour. The school is based at Glandford, ✆0263.741172.

WIVETON

The stone bridge near Wiveton church indisputably marks the head of navigation of the Glaven River, for it was built in 1292 and is still in use. Its creator, William Storm, put a wooden bridge in Cley in the same year, but that has long since rotted.

Wiveton is overshadowed by the popularity of its neighbours, and no modern visitor would ever dream of the village's past glories. But listen to this account of the *Susan*, a *good shippe of burthen...pressed into Queen Elizabeth's service in 1589 for service into Portugal, of which Thomas Coe of Claye went as Quartermaster*. Coe is quoted as claiming that *they have 19 other good shipps some of 140 and one of 160 tons belonging to the same towne, six being built at Wiveton near unto the main channel*.

The church has several recently-discovered masons' marks which show sailing ships of two or three masts, and parish records name actual vessels: Robert Paston had a share in the *Gyles*, while others include the *Gift of God, Trinity, Confidence*, and the *Mary James*. They were fishing boats, merchant vessels, men-of-war, and their rigs included many of the combinations known at the time, from the lateen rig now confined to Arab dhows to the traditional square rig. Purists will know that in strict nautical terms a 'ship' is not a vessel but a style of rigging, with three masts all carrying nothing but square sails.

Harbour dues. An old document states that the *lord of Wiveton Dulcis hath a bushel of coals, salt, or any measurable thing, of every ship that doth unload within the precinct of that manor. There was paid for every English ship, other than those of the same port, 4d (9.6p), for anchorage, and for every alien ship, 8d (19.2p).*

St Mary the Virgin. The parish church, built at the head of the harbour at the end of the 13th cent, now overlooks the village green. A John Hakon wrote in his will of 1437 that he left 200 marks (£132) for 'þe makyng of a newe chyrche in Wyveton,' but only 60 marks (£40) if temporary repairs were done; the churchwardens opted for the complete rebuild. The letter þ is the old way of writing soft *th*, as in 'the,' and gave rise to the mistake of putting *y*, and so making 'ye,' which never existed. The character survives in modern Icelandic, and you'll find it again in the Paston Letters.

But back to Hakon's bequest. As an indication of how large it was, in 1482 the ship-owning Robert Paston bequeathed 8d (3.5p) 'for the bells,' and two years later his widow left 6d for their repair. Paston, who was a member of the letter-writing family, also gave money for the repair of the Chapel of the Holy Trinity on the bridge, and if you look carefully at the bridge's south-west corner you may see evidence of some other building. Another will left money for candles to be lit in front of the statue of Our Lady on the bridge.

Orphan boy. A legend tells of the baby boy found on the village green in the early 16th cent, who was brought up by the entire community so no one family should bear the expense. The lad was given the name Greneway and baptised Raulf. The legend ends with Greneway becoming a rich merchant and founder of the Greneway Charity which left 200 marks to provide 13 poor people of the parish with a penny (0.4p) and a loaf each Sunday 'for ever.'

The charity exists, but the legend of the orphan was wrong. Raulf Greneway was the son of a local farmer and merchant, and his brass in the church has his family arms, the Grocers' Company arms, and his merchant's mark. And nearby is the charity chest in which the Greneway marks were kept. Chest and charity both date from 1558, the year of Greneway's death and of the keeping of the parish records.

CLEY NEXT THE SEA

The church of St Margaret of Antioch is at the southern tip of Cley, overlooking the village green and surprisingly close to Wiveton Church. Blakeney Church is plainly visible, and you can catch a glimpse of Glandford Church to the south, yet another example of how the parish churches of Norfolk dominate the landscape.

Moving village. Here is another example of a wandering village. A major fire on 1 September 1612 destroyed 117 houses clustered around 'Claie' church, although nobody was killed. As the Glaven was already beginning to silt up, the replacement homes were a little to the north, with further growth taking the village ever northward, following the retreating tidal creek.

Church. The church is impressively large for today's small village, the nave and side chapels being about 65ft (20m) wide by 115ft (35m) long, plus 28ft (7.5m) to the altar rail. The tower is short because it belonged to the previous church on this site and was the last part to be built, around 1200 (the chancel was rebuilt around 1250); its base is therefore the oldest part of the present structure.

Sir John de Vaux had been granted 'Cly' manor in 1265; as he already held Boston in Lincolnshire, at that time England's second-largest port, he presumably travelled between the two by boat. Maritime trade was already swelling the population of Cley and, after de Vaux's death in 1288, his two daughters decided to rebuild the church. They commissioned John Ramsey, master mason on Norwich Cathedral, and his nephew William.

Ramsey decided to keep only the original chancel, and in 18 years of intermittent work he produced most of the masterpiece still evident today; the cinquefoil (five-clover-leaf) windows of the clerestory (the upper walls of the nave) are based on what other members of the family had carved for the Palace of Westminster.

When Lady Petronella de Nerford, de Vaux's elder daughter, died in 1326, John Ramsey retired and the proposed new tower was abandoned. Nephew William Ramsey took command of the work, added the north aisle, and completed the project shortly before the

Signatures of some Norfolk worthies: Nelson Brontë; Sir Thomas Gresham; and Sir Edward Coke, builder of Godwick.

Houghton Hall was the home of Britain's first Prime Minister, Sir Robert Walpole. Blickling Hall (below) has associations with Anne Boleyn, but she never lived in this stately home.

Hunstanton's red and white cliffs face west. Sandringham House is a
beautiful country home set amid splendid gardens.

Black Death of 1348, which killed both Ramseys.

South Porch. The south porch, added after the Black Death, is a masterpiece of the stonemason's art, holding 16 armorial crests, including those of John de Vaux, his daughters' husbands, Roger Mortimer the Earl of March, and several saints. And, in the porch roof, a carving of an old woman throwing her distaff at a fox that has stolen a chicken. Look around in the nave and you'll find other miniature treasures in stone.

Bonnie Prince James. Away from the church and out at sea, Cley seamen captured a Scottish ship in March 1406, taking Prince James of Scotland, the 11-year-old son of King Robert III, to France. As England and Scotland were temporarily not warring, the prince was sent on to London where Henry IV merely held him hostage, although the news of this act killed King Robert.

Kidnapping and piracy have never been far removed from the more legitimate affairs of Norfolk seamen. The *Norfolk Chronicle* reported on 16 December 1824:

Thursday and Friday last, were seized on the beach and afloat, by the officers of His Majesty's Customs at this port (Cley), 120 half-ankers of geneva, 19 bags of tobacco, 10 bags of snuff, 10 boxes of segars, and two Chinese ornaments.

The same paper reported in February 1883 a gunfight at Weybourne between smugglers and customs men, who seized six carts holding 127 half-ankers of brandy and 3,500lb (1,600kg) of tobacco.

Modern Cley. Cley today is a beautiful village troubled only by a narrow main street and a very tight corner, which can cause traffic problems. Along this main street is **Made in Cley,** a group of five potters and a jeweller who make their wares on the premises and accept commissions for special orders; ✆0263.740134.

Cley Mill. Nearby is the much-photographed Cley Mill, begun in 1713. The best-known miller here was the last one, Steven Barnabus Borroughs, who worked it from 1840 to 1919 – 79 years. In 1921 it was converted into a holiday home, with the latest renovation in 1983; it was caught in the 1953 floods, losing much of its furniture in the ebb tide.

The mill itself is open to visitors daily Easter-Sep, 1400-1700, for £1, and open for B&B Mar-early Jan; it has three bedrooms for guests, with the original stables now serving as self-catering apartments; ✆0263.740209.

Have a look at the front wall of the Post Office, which appears to be built of broken horse and cattle bones.

Beach. Cley's beach is mainly shingle, and there's a pay car park. On the roadside a mile east of Cley is a chalet owned by the Norfolk

Naturalists' Trust for observing migrating birds; there's a car park nearby. It's also the visitor centre for Cley Marshes and is open Tues-Sun Apr-Oct 1000-1700, issuing permits for the marshes. In winter permits are available at Watcher's Cottage 100m west, and the NNT has offices at 72 Cathedral Close, Norwich, NR1 4DF.

GLANDFORD

Don't come this far without visiting Glandford, which takes its name from one of the most picturesque fords in Norfolk. At the end of World War II the county had hundreds of fords on minor roads, most of which have succumbed to progress. Glandford is different. The ford over the Glaven is around 100ft (30m) wide, and too deep for ordinary cars to cross; the bridge is for pedestrians only.

All but one farmhouse and a few cottages of the village was rebuilt early in the 20th cent by Sir Alfred Joddrell of Bayfield Hall, a mile to the south. He even rebuilt the church.

Baby church. St Martin's Church was in ruins in 1730. In 1875 the chancel was restored, and in 1882 the cemetery reopened. Then along came Sir Alfred who demolished all but the chancel and rebuilt it to his own design, beginning in October 1899 and finishing in August 1906.

But this is no ordinary church. Its diminutive size, particularly noticeable from inside, gives it the appearance of an oversized doll's-house. Yet it has everything that a 17th-cent parish church could have: a hammerbeam roof, a rood screen, carved angels on the pulpit and the corbels in the ceiling – all fashioned in great detail from local oak and cedar. The woodcarvers were Walter Thompson and Frank McGinnty who were so pleased with their work that they carved each other at opposite ends of the frieze above the pew behind the door.

There is a carillon of 12 bells which rings out with the Westminster chimes every hour, and plays hymn tunes at 1200, 1500, 1800 and 2100.

Shell Museum. As you walk up to the church you pass the Shell Museum beyond a lawn on your left. Sir Alfred built this in 1915, and is responsible for some of the impressive exhibits, which include sea shells and allied material from around the world – much of it now on the 'protected species' list. Here is a walking-stick made from a shark vertebrae, a giant tortoise carapace, a giant clam, a nautilus shell with delicate writing on it, and lapidary from Britain and the tropics.

The museum is open Mon-Thur 1000-1230, 1400-1630, Fri-Sat, afternoon only, for 40p.

A mile south, on the Bayfield Hall Estate, is **Natural Surroundings,** where Ann Starling sells plants that attract butterflies and helps you go gardening organically with herbs, flowers and trees. Established 1989 and open daily 1000-1730; ✆0263.711091. Nearby, English Country Cottages has some self-catering holiday homes.

5: **WALSINGHAM and FAKENHAM**

Holy Norfolk

WALSINGHAM IS ENGLAND'S NATIONAL SHRINE. In medieval times it was the most important pilgrimage site in northern Europe, rivalling Santiago de Compostela in north-west Spain and even Rome itself. In modern times, when religion has a smaller role in daily life, Walsingham has again become an important place to go on pilgrimage, or to visit as a tourist and see other people on their pilgrimage. It cannot equal the vast crowds that visit Lourdes, Fâtima in Portugal, or Knock in Ireland, but it attracts tens of thousands of visitors each year. And if you're looking for the place on the map, try *Little* Walsingham; Great Walsingham is a mile away and considerably smaller.

Richeldis de Faverches. Lady Richeldis de Faverches, pious owner of the manor of Walsingham, was at prayer one day when she had a vision of the Virgin Mary. Then, in a dream or trance, she was taken to Nazareth of a thousand years earlier and shown the House of the Annunciation, the simple home where Mary had heard she was to have a baby and where she and Joseph had raised Jesus. Lady Richeldis had the vision twice more, eventually convincing her that she was to build a replica of Christ's home here in Walsingham.

Lady Richeldis ordered a small timber-built chapel and wanted it erected between two wells, but the carpenters were prevented by unseen forces from following her wishes. She spent the night in prayer, and in the morning found the chapel had been built by divine assistance on another site.

There's one question I cannot answer: how did a woman with a French name become lady of the manor five years before the Norman Conquest?

Pilgrimage. While the Fransiscans built their friary at the south end of the village, Elizabeth, the Countess of Clare (Suffolk), and granddaughter to Edward I, founded the Augustinian Priory of St Mary in 1347 on the site of Lady Richeldis's original chapel. Both orders worked to serve the needs of the pilgrims who had learned of

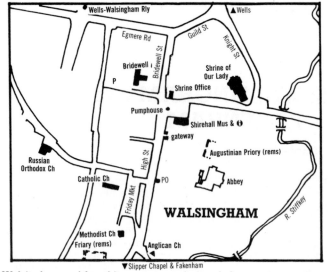

Walsingham and found it more convenient and cheaper to come here than make the hazardous journey to the real Nazareth. Soon, indeed, Walsingham became known as 'England's Nazareth,' and drew a steady stream of visitors from around the country and from other northern lands.

Look at the Ordnance Survey map and trace the tracks those pilgrims made from the port of Lynn, via Hillington, Harpley, and West Barsham, going through today's Sculthorpe Airfield. Even more distinct is the route from Heacham harbour through Sedgeford, Docking, Stanhoe, and across country straight to Walsingham shrine, and there are other routes from Burnham Thorpe, from Wells, and from Blakeney. Many miles of these ancient paths have evolved into the tarred roads of modern times.

Henry III made a pilgrimage to the **Priory of Bromholm** at Bacton in 1233 as, ten years earlier, the priory, an extension of Acre Castle, had claimed to have a fragment of the True Cross. True or not, the publicity was good, as the Miller's Wife in the *Canterbury Tales* calls: 'Helpe, Holy Cross of Bromholm!' Wymondham Abbey and several other places have made the same claim, but the abbots of Walsingham counterclaimed that among their treasures was a sample of mother's milk from the Virgin Mary. So great was belief in this ridiculous assertion that for ages the Milky Way in the night sky was known as the Walsingham Way! Oh, yes: in 1241 Henry III came to Walsingham, and came back at least 10 more times.

In the balance. Walsingham briefly influenced politics when Edward I and the Count of Flanders signed a treaty of alliance here in 1296, and later could perhaps have kept England a Catholic country. Catherine of Aragon's sons had not survived infancy, so Henry VIII took the desperate measure of making a barefoot pilgrimage to Walsingham to pray for his latest ailing infant son.

The son died. Henry decided it was Catherine's fault and so began his campaign for divorce, which led to the break with Rome and the dissolution of the monasteries, initially affecting all religious orders with an income greater than £200 a year: Walsingham was valued at £391.

Dissolution. The 12th-cent priory was wrecked, but the Countess of Clare's other creation, Clare College in Cambridge, survived. Sub-prior Nicholas Mileham and layman George Guisborough were executed, but perhaps the greatest sacrilege was that the Walsingham Madonna was taken to Chelsea and burned. By 1538 the priory ruins were desecrated and deserted, and the slipper chapel had become a farm outbuilding.

Regeneration. For generations Walsingham was dead. Then in 1829 came the Catholic emancipation, and in 1833 a group of Oxford intellectuals met in the Dean's Study at Hadleigh, Suffolk, to plan the second reformation of Church procedure: it became known as the **Oxford Movement.** Soon, a few pilgrims were returning to Walsingham, even though they found the religious houses in near-total ruin. Only the great arch of the east window remained of the priory; its gardens have now been relaid and the arch is open to the public Apr, Wed; May-July & Sep, Sat, Sun, Wed; Aug, Fri-Mon & Wed; plus bank holidays; 1400-1700, for 50p.

Charlotte Pearson Boyd bought the derelict 14th-cent **Slipper Chapel** in Houghton St Giles, 1.5 miles (2.4km) south-west, in 1896 and began its restoration, which was completed in 1934. Originally the final stopping-place for medieval pilgrims coming from the south, it is now the Catholic National Shrine, holding the small **Holy Ghost Chapel** where votary candles burn in thanksgiving. The chapel is open throughout the day.

Pilgrims began arriving in earnest in 1897, their numbers increasing greatly in the 1920s and continuing until 1934 when 10,000 people came to Walsingham in procession. From then until the outbreak of war pilgrimages were not organised, and they virtually ceased during hostilities, but on 17 May 1945, six days after the German surrender, the US Army Air Force in Norfolk organised the first Mass at Walsingham since the Reformation.

Shrine of Our Lady. Meanwhile, the rate of restoration had accelerated. A duplicate of Lady Richeldis's shrine was built in Buxted, Sussex, in 1887, inspiring the local lad Alfred Hope Patten to devote his life to restoring the Walsingham shrine. He became a priest, was offered Walsingham in 1921, and stayed there until his death in 1958. He achieved his ambition by rebuilding Lady Richeldis's chapel in 1931, discovering the 11th-cent well in the process. The chapel, now called the **Holy House,** holds the Annunciation Altar, featuring a carving showing Mary receiving the news that she is to be the mother of God. This carving, commissioned by Fr Patten, is based on the original priory seal held in the British Museum and is the focal point of religious life in Walsingham and the start and finish of all pilgrimages.

Steps beside the Holy House lead down to the Holy Well where pilgrims are once again baptised, and the walls carry hundreds of small plaques bearing appreciations: *Thanks for healing of brain damage, 1982. For success in exams, 1983. For cure of arthritis after prayer, 1934.*

Pilgrimage Church. In 1938 the Holy House was incorporated in the large Pilgrimage Church, which has 15 side chapels.

Prayers. Mass is held daily at 0730 in the shrine, at 1130 in the chapel in the grounds, and Shrine Prayers are offered at 1800, with intercessions (requests) sent in from all around the world. There are many other prayers in addition, plus the services at the Slipper Chapel, the Methodist and Catholic churches, the parish Church of St Mary and All Saints, and the Russian Orthodox Church in the former railway station. There are summertime candlelight processions at 2015 on Saturdays, but the most spectacular prayers are at the annual **National Pilgrimage** which reaches its climax in the priory gardens each Spring Bank Holiday.

The pump house in Common Place, Little Walsingham, was built in the 16th century.

AROUND WALSINGHAM

Little Walsingham was a small farming community until interest revived in England's Nazareth. The village has adapted to its new role as a major tourist and pilgrimage attraction without ruining its character, and the only new housing is tucked away. A tour of Walsingham on foot could start at the Shrine Church, from where go north along Knight St, passing the **Refectory** of the College of Clergy, a half-timbered 16th-cent house. Left into Guild St, for **Guild House** at the next junction. A right fork leads to Egmere Rd and the terminus of the Wells and Walsingham Railway; there's no station.

Left takes you south into Bridewell St and the open area of **Common Place.** As you enter the Place, on your right is an alley leading to the former **prison,** built in 1787 on the site of a leper hospital, with the bridewell built beside it in 1822: a 'bridewell' takes its name from the jail which stood near St Bride's Well in London, and this one had four treadmills. It's open on random occasions.

Opposite the alley is a 15th-cent building, now a shop, beside which is the **Shrine Office** which arranges pilgrimages and accommodation for pilgrims, ✆0328.820255. The 16th-cent **pump house** is closed, but it can still draw water. At the bottom of Common Place is the **Bull Inn,** dating from the 15th cent, while on the south side, behind the limited parking space, is the **Shirehall Museum** and **Tourist Office.** The museum, ✆0328.820510, holds a courthouse of the time of George III (1760-1820) with a prisoner's cell, and other exhibits on the story of Walsingham. Open Easter-Sep daily, Mon-Sat 1000-1700, Sun 1400-1700 (Oct Sat-Sun only), for 60p. The tourist office (same ✆ and times) is the agency for **guided tours** of the village, Apr-Sep, Wed 1100, Thur 1430, £2.40; for other times contact Scilla Landale, Westgate Farm, ✆0328.820250.

A walk down High Street is like a visit to a living museum of architecture, with styles from the 15th to 18th cents, plus the 13th-cent gateway to the Augustinian Priory. Note, in particular, the Georgian front at number 33.

An opening on the right leads to the **Market Place** and the 15th-cent **Black Lion** hotel. The south end of Market Place rejoins High St by the **Methodist Chapel,** built in 1794, then you are confronted with a Y-fork. Left, Church St leads to the parish church, severely damaged by fire on the night of 14-15 July 1961. The tower and south porch are restored, the remainder rebuilt. Right, the main road leads south to the Slipper Chapel, but a side road takes you to the ruins of the **Fransiscan Friary,** a victim of Henry VIII's megalomania; opening times are shown at the gate.

GREAT WALSINGHAM. Overshadowed by its neighbour, Great Walsingham's Church of St Peter is worth a visit but the main interest is probably **The Textile Centre,** where Sheila Rowse puts her designs onto cloth by the silk screen process. There's also a gift shop and tea-room. Open Easter-Oct Mon-Fri 0930-1730; Sat-Sun, bank hols, 1000-1700; group visits in winter; ✆0328.820009.

BINHAM

Binham, 3 miles (5km) north-east, had a priory that excelled the splendour of the Augustinian Priory at Little Walsingham, and even in decay its ruins are much more impressive, the nave still serving as the parish Church of St Mary.

Peter de Valoines, nephew of William the Conqueror, founded Binham Priory in 1091 as a cell (dependency) of the Benedictine Abbey of St Albans, which makes it 30 years younger than Lady Richeldis's shrine. Henry I endowed the priory around 1104 and the first prior, Osgod, was appointed in 1106, although builders didn't begin on the nave until 1130 and work continued for another 150 years; students of architecture can separate the Norman lower levels from the Early English of the upper storeys.

Siege. In the early 13th cent the Abbot of St Albans dismissed Binham's prior, Thomas, which prompted Thomas's friend Robert Fitzwalter to forge a document which stated that he, as patron, could veto any such dismissal. Fitzwalter then laid siege to the priory in 1212, forcing the monks to starvation level. When King John heard of the troubles he sent an armed force, and Fitzwalter fled.

Within the next generation the monk Alexander de Langley, formerly Prior of Wymondham, drove himself insane through studying too much. The prior flogged him, kept him in solitary confinement, and ultimately buried Alexander's body, still in chains.

Corruption. Richard de Parco was the only honourable prior, in office from 1227 to 1244. He raised a charge on Wells windmill to buy some hassocks, arranged for Great Ryburgh church to feed his monks when the larder was empty, he also reroofed the cloister, built the west front, the most impressive aspect of the priory today, and still had £20 when he left office. Most other priors could be described as petty crooks, with William de Somerton (1317-35 with a break of office) the worst. He sold much of the church plate and squandered the proceeds on experiments to turn base metals into gold: why not just melt down the plate and pretend he had succeeded? He was imprisoned; he escaped, was reinstated, and fled the office in 1335, leaving a debt of £600. By contrast, when Henry VIII demolished the priory in 1540, its annual income was down to £140.

Fall and rise. Henry gave the ruined priory to Thomas Paston in 1542, and the **Paston Letters** record the receipt in 1553 of 13/7½d for rubble from the priory to build a house in Wells. Edward Paston planned to build himself a house at Binham using further stonework, but when falling masonry killed a workman, his companions saw this as an evil omen and all further demolition was abandoned. By 1715 workmen were actually restoring the priory, and in 1809 the enormous windows in the west front were bricked in for safety; surviving etchings suggest that this window had the earliest example of bar tracery (slender stone shafts) in England.

Today, almost all the extensive outbuildings have been reduced to ground level, leaving only the nave intact – but this is extremely impressive and, since it doubles as the parish church, is open every day; it's also home to a colony of pipistrelle bats. The priory belongs to English Heritage, but there is no entrance fee.

English Heritage also owns the stump of the **Market Cross** on the village green. This marks the site of the annual four-day fair for which Henry I granted the charter; it continued until the 1950s.

NORTH ELMHAM

St Augustine brought Christianity to England in 597 – don't confuse him with another St Augustine who lived 354-430 – and became the first Archbishop of Canterbury. St Felix, who landed at Babingley, was the first Bishop of East Anglia, with his cathedral at Dunwich, on the Suffolk coast, from 631. About 50 years later, East Anglia was divided into two dioceses, roughly matching the areas of the North folk and the South folk – Norfolk and Suffolk *(see Harpley)*.

Guthrum. The northern diocese was centred on Elmham – the 'north' came much later – and survived until the height of the main Viking attacks between 841 and 855, and the slaughter of Edward, king and saint, in 870, which left the region in chaos. King Alfred defeated the Danish King Guthrum in 890, and Guthrum, converted to Christianity, made Dunwich his administrative and religious capital.

Around 920 a church was on the Elmham site, the bishopric for East Anglia being reintroduced briefly in 955 with Athulf as its first bishop. In 1071 the Norman Archbishop Lanfranc, deciding that bishops' seats should be in towns, demoted Elmham in favour of Thetford (and Dunwich in favour of Bury St Edmunds), but in 1085 the honour passed to Norwich, where it has stayed.

For centuries the Elmham ruins laid forgotten, called locally the 'Castle Hills.' An amateur digger in 1871 assumed they were 14th cent, but an archaeologist in 1903 suggested they could be Saxon. Further digs in 1962 supported the idea that this was indeed Elmham Cathedral, and excavations across the road (not open to the public) in 1967 exposed a Saxon cemetery and village. Still later work has dated the masonry to between 1090 and 1120, *after* the cathedral moved to Thetford, and documentary evidence now tells us that the Saxon cathedral which Lanfranc demoted, was built of wood. So – welcome to North Elmham's Bishop's Chapel, with additional work done in the early 14th cent.

Peasants' Revolt. Henry le Despenser, appointed Bishop of Norwich in 1370, helped to suppress the Peasants' Revolt in 1381 and, as a Royal favour, was granted permission to convert the chapel at Elmham into a moated and fortified house for his private use, ostensibly as a hunting lodge. He scattered many human skeletons in the process, but his work on the chapel preserved the Norman masonry from almost certain destruction. When he died in 1406 the chapel-cum-manor house was abandoned until the Ministry of Works stopped the decay in 1948.

The Bishop's Chapel is now under English Heritage control, with free and unrestricted access.

St Mary's Church. Immediately beside the chapel ruins is the elegant parish church, its oldest part being stones in the chancel belonging to the chapel that Bishop de Losinga built when he moved the diocesan seat. The chancel was in ruins by 1277, but was restored in 15th-cent Perpendicular style. The tall tower is in three stages, and for 25p you can climb it, for an excellent view across country. Now here's an oddity: the church – which means the font – is dedicated to St Mary, but the south chapel is for St James and the north chapel for St John. Multiple dedications such as this infer the church was important.

Vineyard. Elmham Park vineyard occupies the Saxon cemetery site. The 2.6 acre (1ha) vinery is open all year, by appointment only: ✆0362.668571.

BILLINGFORD. Two miles east is Billingford, site of a Roman settlement on the road from Caister to Castle Acre, and a major crossing of the River Wensum in Saxon times. The *Billinga* family was the founder of the royal house of Saxony, and was prominent in the 11th cent.

Signatures of more worthies with Norfolk connections: Edward VII; Queen Anne; Anne Boleyn; Charles, Viscount Townshend.

North Elmham Cathedral? No, it's the ruined Bishop's Chapel.

FAKENHAM

Fakenham was a slow grower, although it began as a 6th-cent Saxon village. It had a market since 1250, and in 1784 Messrs Gurney, Birkbeck, Buxton and Peckover established a bank on the Market Place, but it took the coming of the two railways to make the town expand.

The banking quartet didn't confine themselves to Fakenham; Gurney was busy in Harwich, and Peckover had interests in Wisbech, where Peckover House is now National Trust property. Peckover was a Quaker and so used the Quaker Chapel in Quaker Lane – and there's another lane of that name in Wisbech.

Fire destroyed most properties on the Market Place in 1738, with the Crown Inn replacing a hunting lodge used by the Duke of Lancaster, John of Gaunt (Ghent), former lord of the manor.

The Church of Sts Peter and Paul is probably on a Saxon site, but it was not mentioned in Domesday; the doorway in the west of the north aisle is the oldest part, dating from early Norman times. The nave and chancel were built in the 15th cent, and from 1547 the patronage of Fakenham's church has rested with Trinity College, Cambridge.

If you find one of the churchwardens you may get permission to climb the 146 steps in the tower, 115ft (35m) tall. Then, back at ground level, you may find the poor box with the date 1665 carved on it. The box was thrown out or stolen at some unrecorded time, and discovered in 1888 in a local brewery.

The cemetery, in the north of the town, has a granite memorial to Sir George Edwards (1850-1933), local magistrate, Labour Member of Parliament, and founder of the National Union of Agricultural Workers. Opposite the cemetery is the town's first school, built in 1839, with Constitution Hill, beside it, leading west to the oldest Post Office collection box for miles around.

Gasworks Museum. At the south of town, by the river, one of the oldest gasworks in the country is now the Museum of Gas and Local History, open Tues and Thurs in August, and occasional other dates, 1000-1600; ✆0328.851696. The place produced coal gas from 1846 to 1965, when North Sea gas made it redundant.

Tourist information. The tourist office is at Red Lion House, Market Place, ✆0328.851981.

The THURSFORD COLLECTION

Young George Cushing went from Thursford to King's Lynn in 1920 to see the amusement fair known as the Mart. He was so spellbound at the music and lights, and at the steam engines which generated them that, some years later, he bought a second-hand steam engine and hired it out. He kept buying them, especially when petrol ousted steam and the giant traction engines were going at scrap value; he didn't care that some people thought he was crazy.

More years passed. Steam engines became a novelty and their price soared. George started steam rallies and the crowds came pouring in. Eventually, George's bizarre fleet became the Thursford Collection, based in the farm where he had stored those early machines. In 1977 the collection became a charitable trust for the preservation of steam – it claims to be the world's best – and added fairground and farming ancilliaries such as Wurlitzer and other organs, static steam engines, and a fairground merry-go-round.

Christmas carols. When the Wurlitzer came in 1976 from the Paramount Cinema in Leeds, it needed a special building to house it, as the roundabout did two years later. Reginald Dixon, who had played another Wurlitzer at Blackpool's Tower Ballroom for 40 years, came to play on this organ at Thursford; now a resident organist gives concerts every afternoon in the season, as well as the Christmas carol concerts which began in 1977 and now attract 50,000 people a year – and were seen on national television in 1991.

A steam loco built in 1898 for the Dinorwic slate quarries in Wales now draws a passenger train around the Thursford grounds on a 20in (50.8cm) gauge railway, and visitors can browse through sweet shops and gift shops, a tea room and a picture gallery.

The collection is open daily Apr-May, Sep-Oct, 1300-1500; Jun-Aug, 1100-1700, £4.20; ✆0328.878477.

PENSTHORPE WATERFOWL PARK

A mile east of Fakenham, Pensthorpe Waterfowl Park and Nature Reserve occupies 200 acres (80ha) of wetland and former gravel pits on the north bank of the Wensum. A registered charity, it claims to have one of the world's largest collections, by species, of waterfowl, listing more than 120, of which 100 have bred here.

They include king eiders from the Arctic, pygmy geese from the tropics, and the only torrent ducks outside South America. You can also see avocets and ruffs, species driven to extinction but reintroduced since the last war.

The reserve was begun in 1982, after 1,000,000 tons of gravel were scooped out between 1974 and '79, and bird ringing began in that first season. In the next five years Pensthorpe ringed more wigeon than any other British station, and showed that these birds nested as far away as the River Ob in northern Siberia.

Woodland and wetland at Pensthorpe provide habitats for other creatures such as tits and owls, bluebells and marsh orchids, butterflies and dragonflies, shrews and stoats, and many more.

The **Wetland World Education Centre** has videos explaining the three nature trails, brass engravings of birds suitable for making 'rubbings,' and microscopes for examining feathers; schools are particularly welcome. The Duke of Edinburgh, a prominent conservationist, opened the Courtyard Restaurant in 1988.

Pensthorpe is open daily Apr-Oct, San-Sun Nov-Dec, 1100-1700, for £3.50; ✆0328.851465.

Cromer Church seen from the High Street.

Little Snoring's Church of St Andrew is unique. The tower is round, it is Saxon, and it is freestanding. And in the nave there is a museum to the Royal Air Force.

Between Thursford and Fakenham lies Little Snoring, with its Great twin to the north. The name comes from a Saxon invader or settler named 'Swift, Alert' – *Snear* – and is a source of modern fun, like those other villages of Spital-in-the-Street, Parson Drove, and Mavis Enderby (Lincs), and St Just in Roseland (Cornwall).

Little Snoring's Church of St Andrew is not only intriguing, it's unique. Its small *round* tower is Saxon, probably built around 1010, and it stands separate from the rest of the church: there are freestanding *square* towers at West Walton (Norfolk) and Beccles (Suffolk). The tower still has centuries-old dovecotes at its top, reminders of the time when meat was so scarce in winter that pigeons and doves were bred for the table.

The nave also predates the Norman Conquest, but most of the remainder of the church is from around 1240, and the organ was built around 1800 by an amateur in Fakenham who cannibalised other organs. Restored in 1987 for £2,500, the organ is now recognised as of national significance. The single bell was cast in 1770, so the two earlier bells were sold in 1772.

Another surprise awaits you at the west end of the nave, behind the elevated pews which are in themselves a rarety; four wooden notice-boards from nearby **RAF Little Snoring,** an airfield from the latter years of World War Two. Records of decorations begin with Sgt Rosenbloom of 115 Sqn who got the Distinguished Flying Medal in August 1943, and end with Warrant Officer Smith of 23 Sqn who got the Distinguished Flying Cross in March 1945. A second board lists the enemy planes damaged and destroyed.

BALE

You're too late to see the celebrated **Bale Oak,** in the village of Bale or Bathley, 2 miles (3km) north-east of Thursford. The oak had a circumference of 36ft (10.9m) at human waist level, and its longest branch stretched 75ft (23m) when the tree was felled in 1860. It was condemned to death because the parish officers refused to accept responsibility if anybody were injured by the rotting branches. The lord of the manor, Sir Willoughby-Jones, organised the felling, and had the timber hauled to Cranmer Hall in Fakenham in great procession, with flags and bunting waving. Somewhere, somebody counted the rings and estimated the tree was 1,000 years old.

Stories claim that 20 people could stand inside the hollow trunk; a cobbler made it his home one summer, and another time people kept pigs there.

The Bale Oak is believed to be the last relic of a Celtic or Saxon sacred grove, with All Saints' Church being built beside the tree to preserve the holy link; the only stained glass in the church shows oak leaves and acorns. The National Trust bought a small oak coppice beside the church in 1919, and the site of the celebrated oak now has a notice:

> Here I stand all in disgrace,
> Once the wonder of this place.
> My head knocked off, my body dead,
> And all the virtue of my limbs is fled.

There's another notice in the church. It has no connection with the oak, but is interesting for its possible libellous content:

> Be it Remember'd That Thos Gay, bought of Lucy Clarke, with Bale Town Money which Sum was Sixteen Pounds Ten Shillings, A piece of Land laying in Wells...This Money was given by James Ringall to Buy Blankett to Clad the Poor of Bale, many Years Since. Anno 1774.

THE GHOST VILLAGE

Five miles (8km) south of Fakenham is the deserted village of **Godwick.** All that remains is part of a large Tudor barn now incorporated into a modern building, and the skeleton of the church tower. Since the Industrial Revolution, more than 200 Norfolk villages have died, but Godwick is the only one to have *anything* visible: all the others were ploughed over.

The Saxons settled here, and Godwick thrived until the Middle Ages, but a series of poor harvests on this heavy boulder clay brought an end to the community around 1600.

Yet in 1585 Sir Edward Coke, Chief Justice to Elizabeth I and a member of the family which built Holkham Hall, bought Godwick Manor for £3,500 and created an elegant manor house amid the dying village. Sir Edward had recently married Bridget Paston, but she died in 1598 and is buried at Tittleshall; four months later Sir Edward married the young and wealthy widow of Sir William Hatton, but this second bride insisted on keeping her title of Lady Hatton. She didn't like Godwick, preferring her London home on the site of today's Hatton Garden.

The tower of Godwick's 13th-cent church, demolished soon after Coke built the hall, was left as a folly, an oversized garden ornament. But the house itself died, and was pulled down in 1962.

The site is unfenced, but you are welcome daily 0930-sunset Apr-Sep; park in the farmyard at the end of the approach road.

TITTLESHALL. Less than a mile across the fields, or two road miles away, is the thriving village of Tittleshall. The Church of St Mary the Virgin is unimposing from the outside, yet it contains the tomb and memorial of Sir Edward Coke (see Godwick, above) which cost £400, and the tomb of his wife Bridget Paston, who is shown with the eight of her ten children who survived her. A long plaque lists Coke's achievements, including becoming Speaker of the House of Commons and Lord Chief Justice to James I – and his time in the Tower of London.

There's a memorial to great-grandson Robert Coke, who was grandfather to Thomas William Coke, 'Coke of Norfolk,' KB, Baron of Minster Lovell, Viscount of Holkham, Earl of Leicester, and builder of Holkham Hall. He was the last of the Cokes to be buried here, his funeral procession stretching 2.5 miles (4km), and the nave is overwhelmed by his magnificent memorial. His first wife Jane is also commemorated here, with a carving that cost 3,000 guineas (£3,150) in 1805.

MILEHAM Sir Edward Coke, Godwick's builder, was born at nearby Mileham in 1552. Stigand was lord of the manor here in 1043, when he became Bishop of Elmham. By 1066 he was Archbishop of Canterbury and, as such, crowned Harold, who died at the Battle of Hastings. It was purely the Stigand connection that prompted the Norman invaders to build a castle here, but today only an earth mound remains, on private land behind the village sign.

6: CROMER and AYLSHAM

Disappearing Norfolk

IF YOU WERE TO STAND on the clifftop on the northern edge of Muckleburgh Camp, where the Muckleburgh Collection is, you could locate to within a few hundred yards the point where Norfolk ceases growing and starts disappearing. To the west, helped by the man-made shingle bank which protects Cley Marshes, the land has advanced into the sea. But to the east, the sea is steadily wearing away the land, and has advanced untold miles since the Ice Ages. West: the beaches are wide, giving way to the vast mudflats in The Wash. East: the beaches are good but narrow as the sand is continually being washed away, either towards Hunstanton or to the Gunfleet Sands off Clacton. That's why the 18th-cent adage grew up:

He who would Old England win
Must at Weybourne Hope begin

– because here the sea was deep enough to allow an invading army to disembark directly onto the beach.

CROMER

The sea had claimed the church of **Shipden-juxta-Mare** by 1390, so the people decided to build another in Shipden-juxta-Felbrigg on land that Edward III had given them. As the area was also known as Crowmere, the community that grew up around the church took the name of Cromer.

Church. The Church of Sts Peter and Paul was completed during the reign of Henry IV – 1399-1413 – its tower at 160ft (48.7m) being the tallest in Norfolk, dwarfed only by the magnificent spire of Norwich Cathedral at 315ft (96m), which in turn is England's second-tallest spire, beaten only by the one at Salisbury which reaches 404ft (123m).

Bow bells? The church prospered for a mere century until Henry VIII's actions over the monasteries cut off further investment in things religious. An inventory of 1552 recorded that the five bells, weighing 62cwt (3,149kg), were valued at £46.10s (50p). In 1681 the chancel had decayed so badly that the rector of Ingworth received permission from the Bishop of Norwich to demolish it with gunpowder. By 1757

Lord Leicester of Holkham Hall built this sea wall at Wells in 1859.

the roof of the nave and aisles had collapsed, restricting services to the base of the tower. The finances were so desperate that in 1767 the Bishop of Norwich raised £332 by selling the brasses and the lead from the church roof, replacing it with slates, as well as selling four of those five bells: 52cwt at £3.16.0d per cwt for £197.12.0d (2,641kg for £197.60p). Legend claims they were sent by sea to their new home in St Mary le Bow Church, near St Paul's Cathedral, which would mean they became the famous Bow Bells, and anybody born within hearing of them is, by definition, a Cockney. Sadly, the Whitechapel Foundry belies the story as its records prove it cast the bells for St Mary le Bow and St Mary atte Bow.

Today Cromer church has six bells with a total weight of 2 tons 9cwt 9lb (2 tonnes, 493kg), and a sign on the belfry, which you pass on your way up the tower, adds that the bell metal is 77% copper, 23% tin.

Harry Yaxley. At the 90th of the 171 steps up the tower is a small opening called Harry Yaxley's Hole, named from the boy who was dangling from this opening while he collected birds' eggs, his legs held by a friend inside the tower. When the friend chose that moment to demand a greater share of the yield, Harry called back: "You shan't hev 'em."

"Then I'll drop you," said the friend.

"Drop away, then," Harry replied, and reached the ground somewhat quicker than he had expected. He survived.

Life expectancy. Other people in Cromer and Sheringham seem

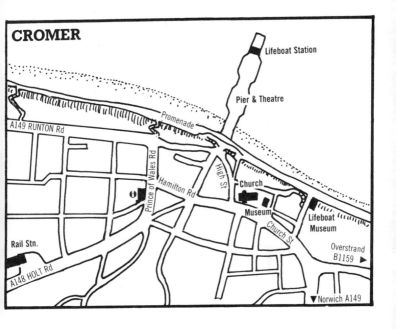

GLORIA DEO IN EXCELSIS says the wording in the parapet at Felbrigg Hall.

to defy death, as recent research has shown that life expectancy here is noticeably greater than the average figure for Britain. By contrast, Lowestoft has the country's highest incidence of Huntington's chorea, a killer disease passed on through the male line.

Crabs. Cromer grew slowly, and was purely a fishing village until the unwelcome railway began bringing tourists. As it has no harbour, all the boats were launched from the beach and hauled into the town when storms threatened. Despite this inconvenience, Cromer developed a reputation for supplying the best crabs in the country.

Museums. The **Cromer Museum,** hiding behind a stone wall on Tucker St, east of the church, is built in fishermen's cottages of Victorian times and preserves the original cooking range and gaslamps. It also tells the story of the crab fishermen, the development of Cromer as a fashionable resort, and of the region's fascinating geology. Open Mon-Sat 1000-1700, Sun 1400-1700 for a fee; ℰ0263.513543. The **Lifeboat Museum,** by the disused No 2 Lifeboat Station, is open daily May-Sep 1000-1600 and occasionally out of season; donations.

Lifeboat. Not surprisingly, it tells the story of the Cromer lifeboats, beginning with No 1's first call-out on 3 December 1867 to the Brixham brig *Wild Rose,* and No 2's first call on 9 April 1868. No 2 station closed on 22 June 1967, and No 1 lifeboat is now launched from the end of the pier.

Henry Blogg. The town's most famous lifeboatman is Henry Blogg, who joined the service in January 1894 aged 18, and retired 53 years 9 months later, in September 1947, having been the coxwain (captain) for 37 years 7 months. He won the George Cross, the British Empire Medal, the RNLI gold medal three times, the silver medal four times, the Canine Defence League silver medal, and the Queen of The Netherlands presented him with a gold watch. He died in 1954.

From 1935 to 1945 he coxed the *H.F.Bailey,* which answered 128 calls and saved 518 lives; Peter Cadbury of the chocolate company bought the boat in April 1991 and presented it to the Lifeboat Museum where it now stands on permanent display.

The resort. Cromer is a pleasant and picturesque town, with a good shopping area, some splendid gardens and several quaint backstreets around the church. Its pier was damaged in 1953 and 1989, but has been repaired; the **Pavilion Theatre** at the end has a reputation for attracting top-class performers in the summer, providing the town's main entertainment. As the beach is mostly sandy and good for building castles, Cromer is suitable for young children and for adults who like relaxation – the Royal Cromer Golf Club has an 18-hole course – but the absence of discos and night clubs rules it out for teenagers. The town **carnival** is around the last week in May, and the **tourist office** is in the old bus station on Prince of Wales Rd,

Geology. The cliffs between Bacton and Weybourne attract geologists from around the world as they show some of the best cross-sections of terminal moraines in the world: the rubbish that glaciers brought down from Scotland and Scandinavia and dumped here at the end of the Ice Ages.

The layer of **Weybourne Crag** holds around 50 species of shells, while the several **Forest Bed** deposits yield bones of hippopotamus, hyena, elephant, beaver, musk ox and whale, creatures of the tropics, the arctic, and the oceans. Elsewhere you might find trunks and roots of trees that were uprooted from dry land where the North Sea now is.

Chalk. All of East Anglia, and south-east England except The Weald, stands on a bed of chalk, which outcrops in Hunstanton cliffs, the Chiltern Hills, and the Downs of Kent and Sussex. Several parts of Norwich are built over chalk mines which have collapsed in recent years, swallowing houses and a double-deck bus. Drilling in Norwich has proved the chalk to be 1,150ft (350m) thick, and estimates put it at around 1,500ft (450m) under Cromer, probably the thickest layer anywhere in the world.

OVERSTRAND. Overstrand – the name means 'above the beach' – is a satellite village to the east. There is no promenade, no entertainment, and access to the good beach is down steep paths, provided as if by afterthought. The village has many retirement homes, and coastal erosion is a continual threat. The 14th-cent church

Wells-next-the-Sea was Wells-under-the-Sea during the East Coast Floods. The museum and the tide measure are in the centre background.

vanished over the cliffs ages ago, so St Martin's is an 18th-cent replacement, restored in 1911.

WEST RUNTON. Caravan sites, with a few campsites, occupy some of the clifftop between Cromer and West Runton, with others tucked into the hills formed by the terminal moraine. The **beach** is sandy to the east, shingly on the west, with a large pay-car-park in the middle. Holy Trinity Church serves both East and West Runton, its 13th-cent tower being the oldest part. The remainder of the church collapsed in the 14th cent and has been rebuilt.

NORFOLK SHIRE HORSE CENTRE

West Runton's main attraction is the Shire Horse Centre and Countryside Collection on the south edge of the village. David and Jonquil Bakewell opened the centre in 1982 as a working museum and a showplace for draught horses, not as a commercial farm; the only crops grown are grass and cereals, for fodder.

Daily at 1115 and 1500, Sun-Fri plus bank holiday Sat, Apr-Oct, one or more of the centre's horses is harnessed to the appropriate equipment to give a two-hour demonstration of what life on the land was like before the 1950s when mechanisation sent most horses to the slaughter house. In addition, a calendar of special events offers ploughing, drilling, harrowing, shoeing, hay tedding (raking), the corn harvest with an old-style binding machine, a foal parade, and demonstrations of sheep dogs at work – all subject to weather and other factors. Adult's admission is £3; ✆0263.75339.

The outbuildings include a gift shop, museum of farm equipment, smithy, video room, and ♿ toilets as well as the stables for draught horses and ponies.

The Bakewells explain the origins of the various breeds of heavy horse: the shire, which can weigh more than a ton; the Suffolk punch, now desperately rare; the Clydesdale; the Percheron, bred in France and introduced here after World War One. Jonquil Bakewell has collected representatives of Britain's ponies: the Shetland, Highland, Fell, Dales, Welsh, Exmoor, New Forest and Dartmoor, as well as the Connemara from Ireland.

Additionally, children can ride around the village in a horse-drawn cart, and there's the **West Runton Riding School** open all year, with the option of going on an escorted pony-trek in the glacial hills.

SHERINGHAM

When early Britons were digging flints from Grime's Graves near Brandon, their compatriots were living on the glacial hills of Beeston Regis, south of Sheringham. A thousand years later, the Romans built kilns here for firing pottery, and 1,000 years after that, the Domesday Book demanded by William I as a detailed survey of England and its

(Map labels: Lifeboat Stn, 'Marble Arch', Promenade, Henry Ramer Upcher, LB, Two Lifeboats pub, Esplanade, Westcliff, Craft Centre (ex LB house), P, Wyndham St, Augusta St, White hall Yd, P, High St, Co-Op St, St Peter's Ch, Clock Tower, Museum, PO, Cremer St, Church St, Station Rd, N.N.Rly Stn, P, B.R. Stn, CROMER Rd A149)

wealth, mentioned a church which was to become All Saints', Upper Sheringham, in the area still known as 'Upper Town.'

By 1197 the Augustinian Priories at Beeston Regis and **Weybourne** (both now in ruins) were serving pilgrims for Walsingham, but the main occupation was fishing, with boats being launched from the beach midway to Weybourne. Fish merchants moved here in the 14th cent, establishing themselves around what is the heart of the modern town; from 1358 they were granted a licence to trade into Blakeney.

Sheringham has never had a harbour, which was a disadvantage even when boats were smaller, but the fishing industry was gradually establishing a solid community that needed a better church, so in 1452 **All Saints'** was rebuilt, the south porch being added in the 15th cent; but records still name the rectors as far back as 1322.

Fishing. An early 16th-cent tax, levied on all fishing boats working out of Sheringham, led to detailed records being kept, which tell us that in 1591 the town had 17 full-time and five part-time boats. Later records show around 200 here, but overcrowding forced several craft to migrate across to Lincolnshire. A recently-restored **smokehouse** at the east end of Wyndham St probably had a dual use as a storehouse for smugglers.

Inevitably, the town developed its own boatbuilding industry, which gave Sheringham its two privately-owned lifeboats. In 1838 the Hon. Mrs Charlotte Upcher of Sheringham Hall gave the *Augusta*, named from her youngest daughter; the 33ft 6in (10.2m) 16-oar boat was stored in a special building (now gone) on West Cliff from 1838 to 1894, and ended its days at Ranworth Broad, its bows ultimately becoming a garden shed. The family's replacement boat, *Henry Ramey Upcher,* launched in September 1894, continued in service until 1935, saving around 200 lives in that time. It was last launched to celebrate the defeat of Japan in 1945 and now rests in its original boathouse near West Cliff. The Upcher family has been in the area for generations, as you'll see from the Abbot Upcher monument in All Saints' Church.

The RNLI's old boathouse, built on Lifeboat Plain in 1867, was abandoned because of storm damage to the slipway in 1897; it now holds the **Sheringham Craft Centre,** slotted between the Smuggler's Haunt restaurant and The Crown pub, and selling pottery, jewellery, ceramics and prints. The RNLI's present premises are on West Promenade, open to view during summer.

The *Augusta* is prominently featured on the front of the **Two Lifeboats** pub on High St, the other boat being the RNLI's *Duncan.* The pub is almost 300 years old, many of its timbers having begun their working life aboard ships that were wrecked along this coast. The Upcher family bought the place in 1878 and opened it as the Two Lifeboats coffee house; and from being an 18th-cent brothel it became, in part, a 19th-cent mission hut for bible classes.

Tourism. It was the coming of the railway in 1887 which changed the town's destiny. Tourists arrived. People with smart clothes and plenty of money came by train to visit Sheringham and *do nothing,* to the amazement of the hard-working locals. Soon the Sheringham Hotel and the Grand Hotel were built to satisfy this bizarre demand, with the Burlington Apartments coming in 1899. The Mainsail Haul even attracted the famous, including **Vaugn Williams** who worked on his *Pastoral Symphony* here in 1919, and explorers **Captain Robert Falcon Scott** and **Sir Ernest Shackleton.** Only the Burlington remains, now called a hotel. But before the turn of the century the first banks arrived, the Water Company and the Gas Company were formed: so was the sewage works. The town reservoir had been built back in 1862, enlarged from a drinking fountain dating from 1814; in 1901 a local woman paid for a public clock to go on top of the squat reservoir, so giving the town its distinctive **Clock Tower.**

In 1842 the Upcher family gave the lower town its own fishermen's chapel, but the growing village needed a new church, and by 1895 the aldermen had laid the foundation stone of **St Peter's;** the building, which looks like a theatre topped by a small steeple, cost £8,000 and was consecrated in 1897, forcing the Upcher chapel to close. Strangely, St Peter's did not become the parish church until 1953, forcing another change – the merger of All Saints' with Weybourne.

The oak behind St Peter's Church was horticulturalist Jack Baker's gift to the town to mark the coronation of George V in June 1911; the council's commemorative tree died, probably because of problems in planting it in high summer.

Zeppelin. A German airship made history at 2030 on 19 January 1915 by dropping the first bomb from the air onto British territory. The bomb crashed through the roof of a cottage in Whitehall yard off Wyndham St, and finished in the kitchen, without exploding; the occupier carried it away in a bucket.

Museum. Sheringham's own museum opened in 1990 in a fisherman's cottage down an alley opposite the NatWest Bank on Station Road. Open daily Easter-Sep and weekends in winter, 1000-1600, free, it has displays on fashion, fishing, and local history, backed up by a gift shop. The next cottage down the alley was the home of a washerwoman.

Lavatory. For something unusual, visit the public lavatories in the 'Marble Arch,' the bridge under the esplanade. Where else would you find lavatories with stained glass windows?

The resort. Sheringham is a lively resort without being brash. The beach has a residue of shingle at the top, with good sand exposed on the falling tide. The town has discos, video games rooms, and an amusement arcade, with **Splash,** the tropical leisure pool on Weybourne Rd, offering fun for all the family, plus a fitness club. Opened by the Princess of Wales in May 1988, its hours are complex, so ✆0263.825675 for details.

Jet skis and water skis are permitted, subject to restrictions; call the **tourist office** for details, ✆0263.824329. The office is between the two railway stations.

The Muckleburgh Collection at Weybourne has Britain's largest private collection of military vehicles that's open to the public.

NORTH NORFOLK RAILWAY

Two railway stations? Indeed! As soon as British Rail closed the line from here to Holt and Melton Constable in 1964, appeals went out urging people to join the M&GN Preservation Society. Response was good, but the society struggled for two years before being able to buy the three-mile (4.5km) section to Weybourne, and by then BR had removed all the track from Holt to Weybourne and was approaching Sheringham.

BR pulled out of Sheringham Station in 1967 in favour of a smaller one on the other side of the main road – hence the two stations – allowing the enthusiasts to lease the main building for their head-quarters.

Red tape. On 4 June of that year the railway, soon to be called the **'Poppy Line,'** received its first rolling stock. Work had already begun on relaying the line into Weybourne, but the enthusiasts were meeting continual opposition from a government that did not favour private enterprise. By 1969 the North Norfolk Railway Company was formed and had gone public, raising £14,000 by the sale of shares. The company needed one Light Railway Order to allow it to carry members of the M&GNPS, and a public inquiry followed by a second Light Railway Order, plus numerous inspections of rolling stock and track, before it could carry fare-paying members of the public. This licence came in 1976, allowing the Poppy Line to resume what British Rail had abandoned, but after a break of 12 years.

The enthusiasts have now relaid the track to Holt and operate to a regular timetable, with steam locomotives and restored carriages being the main attraction – but the Poppy Line has several diesel locos for standby duty, or for use when the countryside is tinder-dry.

Enthusiasts giving their time and money help keep the line running, but it has also gained publicity from being used in film and television, notably in the TV series *Hi-de-hi* and *Dad's Army.*

Rolling stock. Rail enthusiasts would presumably like to know that the Poppy Line has two ex-BR locos; a J15 0-6-0 built at Stratford in 1912 and a B12/3 4-6-0 built by Beyer Peacock in 1928. Others include *Pony,* an 0-4-0 of 1912 bought from Blyth Harbour Commissioners; *Fireless,* an 0-6-0 of 1929 run by Procter & Gamble; *Wissington,* a 1938 0-6-0 that British Sugar used; the ex-Coal Board 0-6-0 from Ashington Colliery; the 1940-built *Ringshaw,* an 0-6-0; *Harlaxton,* an 0-6-0 built in 1941 for Stewart & Lloyds; *Birchenwood,* another 0-6-0 of 1944; *12,* an 0-6-0 of 1955 used by the Central Electricity Generating Board; and an 0-6-0 of 1954 used by the National Coal Board. Carriages include one from the old Norfolk Coastal Express, built in 1907, but the oldest stock is a flat wagon from 1890.

Timetable. The timetable is complex, with up to 8 trains daily in each direction in August, tapering down to a minimum of three daily

The North Norfolk Railway began carrying fare-paying passengers in 1976 and is now a firm favourite with visitors to Sheringham.

on half the days in Apr and Oct; there are normally no standard services from Nov to Mar. For general information, including chartering a train, ✆0263.822045; talking timetable, ✆0263.825449.

Sheringham Park. The National Trust now owns Sheringham Park, in Upper Sheringham. The park and woods are open year round, dawn to dusk, for £1.50 car park fee; on foot, it's free. A raised boardwalk for ♿ visitors goes through the rhododendron woods, and there are some good viewpoints, particularly of the Poppy Line. The hall is leased to a tenant, to whom you must apply in writing if you want to see inside.

WEYBOURNE

The deep water of Weybourne Hope, just beyond low water mark, has made this village a potential landing-site for invaders for generations. The first military defence was planned, but not built, in 1588 under the threat of the **Spanish Armada.** An undated entry in the Holt Parish Register comments:

> In this yeare was the town of Wabourne fortified with a continuall garison of men bothe of horse and foote, with skonces [earthworks], ordinaunce and all manner of warlike appoyntment to defend [prevent] the Spannyards landing theare.

The Napoleonic menace prompted a contingent of artillerymen being stationed on the clifftop, but when the army next moved in, in 1939, it came to stay. Pill-boxes (gun emplacements), trenches, and wooden huts for the troops scarred the clifftop for several years, but in 1935 **Weybourne Camp** expanded into a large anti-aircraft gunnery school. In those days the code word for 'A' was *ack,* so anti-aircraft was called *ack-ack,* a name which lingers on in certain quarters. Later 'A' was coded *able,* but it's now known internationally as *alpha.* The ack-ack school fired out to sea at gliders and other towed aerial targets so frequently that it restricted Sheringam's fishermen who were after shells of a different kind.

Churchill. Soon the camp was using catapult-launched pilotless aircraft known as *Queen Bees,* and was experimenting with rockets, the forerunner of today's guided missile. Weybourne was vital to the nation's defences when World War Two broke out, bringing Winston Churchill here on 10 June 1941. Yet the Luftwaffe paid only one visit, on 11 July 1940, when it bombed the camp and the village, with no loss of life.

By the time the last ack-ack gun was fired, on 2 October 1958 – the camp closed soon after – an estimated 250,000 troops had trained here, firing around 1,500,000 shells out to sea. *And here's a note of caution: when walking on the shingle beach, keep a lookout for unexploded shells and sea mines, and report any you find.*

Berry Savory had opened a small military museum in Inveraray Castle, ancestral home of the dukes of Argyll, but needed larger premises for expansion. As the old Weybourne Camp looked ideal he moved down to Norfolk, and the Duke of Argyll performed the opening ceremony in May 1988; the new museum took its name from the nearby hill.

THE MUCKLEBURGH COLLECTION

The collection had around 40 military vehicles on opening day, but it increased that to more than 120 in the first three years, plus more than 1,500 other exhibits, becoming what its owner claims to be the largest private collection of its kind in Britain open to the public – and most of the vehicles have been rebuilt or restored in the workshops on site. Even the old NAAFI (Navy, Army and Air Force Institute) building, which is the nucleus of the display, has been restored to its wartime glory.

Wars. The military hardware on view comes from a wide range of countries, including Belgium, Czechoslovakia, France, Ireland, Israel, Italy, the Netherlands, Norway, Switzerland, and the Commonwealth of Independent States (the old USSR). Theatres of conflict are mainly those in Europe in World War Two, but there are trophies from the

Six-Day War, the Falklands Campaign of 1982, and the Gulf War of 1991.

Weapons. Weapons from those wars start with a Willys Jeep and reach their climax in the Russian T34 tank, including anti-tank guns, field guns, ambulances, armoured personnel carriers, rocket launchers, Ferret and other scout cars – and some Bofors ack-ack guns.

The model room has an extremely wide range of small-scale ground weapons and aircraft, some based on materiel from the First World War. The diorama room re-creates World War Two graphically with personal mementoes, and a glimpse at a Fighter Command airfield as its aircrew 'scramble' to intercept the enemy.

Yeomanry. A special hall remembers the Suffolk and Norfolk Yeomanry, founded in 1782 by Viscount Townshend of Raynham.

The collection is open daily, Apr-Oct, 1000-1700 for £2.60; ✆0263.70210.

Weybourne Priory. The Augustinian Canons came to England in the 11th cent, building their first priory at Colchester. They expanded throughout East Anglia, beginning their priory at Weybourne some time between 1200 and 1216, as a dependency of the West Acre priory. The man behind the project was Sir Roger Meyngaren (now anglicised to Mannering and Mainwaring) whose family had held the manor since 1071.

The priory disagreed with West Acre in the 14th cent and gained some independence, but it was never big enough to stand completely alone, even though it drew some income from Walsingham pilgrims. Indeed, the Bishop of Norwich, making his 'visitation' in 1514, noted that there was only one canon; by 1530, the prior and the last canon had decided the end was in sight and sold everything they could move, leaving only a small copper crucifix. At the next visitation the bishop found a priory that had gone into voluntary liquidation long before Henry VIII thought of demolishing them all. The empty buildings, which gradually collapsed into ruin, passed eventually to Sir John Gresham, founder of the grammar school in Holt, and later to the Walpole family. All that remains today is a large building behind the parish church, its walls ranging from 50ft (15m) high, to scars on the ground. It is not open to the public.

All Saints' Church. The Austin canons absorbed the existing church into their priory and, when the collapse came, the church was dragged down into destitution and ruin. For centuries the parish had no resident priest; it scarcely had a usable church. Then restoration began in 1866, reaching its climax in 1888 when the nave was re-roofed.

Mill. The old windmill, east of the village, has also been restored, but as it's part of a private house, you can't go in. Beside it, a path leads down to the shingle **beach**. A good road from the village centre leads

Gresham's School in Holt has grown enormously since 1900.

to a pay car park by the shingle bank.

KELLING. A mile west of Weybourne, the small village of Kelling slides away to the south. At the crossroads is **Picturecraft Gallery**, a branch of the main gallery in Holt. Here it is open in season Fri-Wed 1000-1700.

The road south passes St Mary's Church, whose list of rectors begins with Robert de Kelling in 1266. **Kelling Aviaries,** a mile to the south, has closed – so now let us jump five miles to the east, to the village of Gresham, whose name probably has some link with 'grass,' hence the grasshopper as the emblem of the village, of the Gresham family, of Gresham's School in Holt and, (via the Royal Exchange) of the now-vanished Martin's Bank.

GRESHAM

William de Warrenne received the Gresham estates soon after the Norman Conquest, and in the reign of Henry III (1216-'72), the village received its charter for a market, a major achievement for any community. Yet Gresham did not expand into a market town, possibly because it was too close to Upper Sheringham. The lack of development saved All Saints' Church from the improvers and it still has its Saxon round tower.

Edmund Bacon, who was squire of Gresham in the early 14th cent, built a fortified manor in 1319 which became **Gresham Castle** and which the Paston family bought in 1429. A Lord Moleyns laid siege to it when the Paston squire, John, was on a business trip in London, and managed to evict Mrs Paston and the servants. Soon after that the castle was abandoned, and now only a few insignificant ruins remain.

Gresham family. The Greshams slowly came to prominence from poor beginnings in the 14th cent. Two centuries later, Sir Thomas Gresham had become a merchant trader and was to be financial adviser to Henry VIII, Edward VI, Mary and Elizabeth. It was he who established the **Royal Exchange** in London, which opened in 1571 although the original building was destroyed in the Great Fire of 1666. But the character who holds our interest is Thomas's brother, Sir John, who moved to Holt, where we shall meet him again.

NORTH BARNINGHAM. As you leave Gresham for Holt, following John's footsteps, you may notice an isolated church at a crossroads – it's at Ordnance Survey grid reference 150372 – and find yourself in the middle of a village that has totally vanished. Understandably, the Church of St Peter is redundant, but keys are available if you want to be inquisitive.

BACONSTHORPE. The Bacon family, seen at Gresham, has obvious connections with Baconsthorpe – *thorpe* means 'village' and comes from the Dutch *dorp* and German *Dorf* – but you'll have to search to find the link. When the font, presented in 1886 to the parish church of St Mary, began subsiding, investigations revealed a highly elaborate coffin under the floor, collapsing under the weight. The coffin is believed to be of one of the Bacon family. Now look up at the centre of the roof for a painted shield bearing an M for Mary and the heads of three pigs. The same three pigs appear in stained glass in the south aisle windows, taken from Baconsthorpe Castle in 1958 to repair damage done by a German bomb in 1941. Is the link apparent?

Heydon. The name most prominent in the church is Heydon; a family which had vast sheep farms in the area in Tudor times; Heydon's coat of arms is the engrailed cross (its edges look chewed) seen on the monument blocking a window in the south aisle, and elsewhere in the church.

The church has two distinct architectural oddities: it is built of *white* flint, which is found only in this part of Norfolk; and the columns supporting the nave roof lean outward very noticeably. This is a design fault, seen in several churches, resulting from the roof sagging in the middle and pushing its edges outwards; elsewhere in the country the builders would have carried this stress to the ground with flying buttresses outside the church.

Baconsthorpe Castle. The Heydon family built the fortified manor house and wool-processing factory which became Baconsthorpe Castle, the ruins of which lie a mile north of the village. The Heydons brought their sheep into the castle through a turnstile at the north end of the 'long room,' where they were shorn. The south end of the room has the remans of the plumbing to a wooden trough, perhaps where the wool was washed, but we do know that the weavers worked on the first floor.

John Heydon began building the castle in the 15th cent; the date is unknown as Heydon, a cunning lawyer with a reputation for cheating, did not apply for the required Royal licence to fortify his property. The Heydon fortunes were at a low level by 1600, and after the Civil Wars of 1642-49, most of the castle was demolished, the gatehouse surviving into the 18th cent as Baconsthorpe Hall. The courtyard served as a walled garden, but is now down to grass.

English Heritage owns the ruins which are always open, with no fee.

Babes In The Wood. Lady Jane Grey, England's queen for 13 days in July 1553, was related to Thomas and Jane de Grey who were orphaned in 1562, aged three and two. Both were made wards of Queen Elizabeth and sent to live with their Catholic stepmother in Baconsthorpe. Both died here, and under the terms of the will their uncle claimed their inheritance, £300 a year for Thomas and a £500 lump sum for Jane. Misfortune soon struck the uncle and he died a pauper.

That's the true story, but legend claims the uncle hired two ruffians to kill the children, whom they abandoned to their fate in Wayland Wood, near Thetford – so giving rise to the story of the Babes In The Wood.

HOLT and GRESHAM'S SCHOOL

John Gresham bought Holt Manor House in 1546 for £170 to convert it into a grammar school. The Letters Patent (a licence granted under the Great Seal of England) of April 1554, permitted one such school in Holt, to be called 'The Free Grammar School of Sir John Gresham, Knight, Citizen and Alderman of London,' for the sole purpose of teaching boys grammar. Sir John endowed the school with land in around 12 parishes, plus three houses in Cripplegate, London; on 16 October 1556 the 'Wardens of the Mistery of Fishmongers' (Sir John had joined the Worshipful Order of Fishmongers) were appointed governors – and a week later Sir John died of the plague.

The Fishmongers opened the school in 1562, with a licence for 30 non-fee-paying boys (plus boarders), to be increased in 1671 to 35.

At this time, almost all teachers were ordained churchmen, and they all needed a licence from the local bishop, who therefore had strict control over what was taught, and how; to check on progress the bishops made irregular 'visitations' much as they did with the monasteries.

Cambridge University. Thomas Tallis, appointed headmaster in 1606, made Sir John Gresham's school one of the best in the eastern counties, sending 24 boys to Caius College, Cambridge, during his 34 years in office. He left his own private books to the school, so providing the nucleus of its library. By the way, John Keys was a Norwich man who changed the spelling (but not the pronunciation) of his name to Caius; in 1353 he rescued the college that Edmund Gonville of King's Lynn had founded in 1348, and it's now called Gonville and Caius.

Civil Wars. The Civil Wars ended on 30 January 1649 with the beheading of Charles I at Whitehall, followed by the abolition of the monarchy. But in 1650 a Royalist uprising in Holt showed that the eastern counties were still opposed to the dictator Oliver Cromwell. On Christmas Day 25 Royalists were executed in Norwich, including William Hobart, brother of the lord of the Manor of Holt, and Thomas Cooper, usher at Holt's grammar school; a legend still claims that Cooper was the headmaster and that he was hanged outside Gresham's school. Squire Edmund Hobart, whose monument is on the south wall of the chancel in St Andrew's parish church, was fined heavily.

Fire. Timber houses under thatched roofs have always been vulnerable to fire, and on 1 May 1708 most of the town of Holt burned down, causing damage valued at £20,000. A historian said the inferno travelled so fast that nobody could save even the meat from the market stalls. The thatched chancel roof blazed, but the molten lead from the nave roof damaged the stone floor so badly that evidence is still visible.

The rebuilt town was a little to the west, around the present market place, but in recent times it has also spread to the east. Gresham's school escaped with minor damage, which the governors repaired in 1729, around the time the church nave was reroofed. This was also the year in which John Holmes was appointed headmaster. Holmes, who was not an ordained priest, made his mark by extending the curriculum to include geography and history, as well as the school drama production; and when he wasn't satisfied with existing textbooks, he wrote his own.

After Holmes, the governors went back to appointing priests to the headship: the man who took office in 1808 soon became vicar of Sheringham and Weybourne as well as head teacher at Holt. It showed. He was a poor teacher, and in his 50 years in the job two rival schools opened in Holt, taking most of his pupils. Between 1857 and '60 Gresham's school revised its curriculum to include arithmetic, geometry, Latin and Greek, and reopened in 1858 – but the next two headmasters were still churchmen.

Gresham's School. Mr Howson, appointed head in 1900, was a teacher from a new mould. In his 19 years in the job he transformed a lacklustre and ailing local school with 44 boys into a public school of national appeal. He taught science, French, and German, he soon abolished the cane, and he saw the classes move into new buildings on the east edge of town, the nucleus of the present school. But most of all, Howson turned the institution into Gresham's *School*, at last with a capital 'S,' without alienating the people of Holt who wanted it to keep its local character.

Sir John Gresham had started a free school for local lads, but by 1630 it was charging £7 a year for fee-paying boarders. By 1988 the nationally-known public school was charging £7,275 a year each for around 470 senior boarders (plus 200 at prep), and employing a staff of 225 who received £2,000,000 a year in salary. In many respects, Gresham's School *is* Holt.

St Andrew's Church. The fire destroyed much of interest in the town, with the church narrowly escaping. It is set at the end of a short avenue of limes, with the churchyard now established as a nature reserve; in addition, jackdaws nest in the tower, and pipistrelle bats breed inside the main building. Memorials include those to John Holmes and Thomas Cooper from the school, William Briggs, physician to William III, and Edmund Hobart who was executed at Norwich.

The modern town has plenty of character in its mock-old buildings and winding alleys. **Picturecraft** has an art gallery in Lee's Courtyard (✆0263.713259) and there's a small **museum** nearby. **Wansbeck Doll's Houses** is in Chapel Yard (✆0263.713933).

Picnic. There's a beautiful picnic spot by a lake in the woods east of Holt. It's at OS grid ref 105390.

Felbrigg Hall is a beautiful home in Jacobean style.

LETHERINGSETT

Early in the 20th cent a blacksmith wrote this bill:

The bill:

Osforarfada 2/–

Afortheos 1/–

Ashuinonim 2/–

Anafechinonimagin 1/–

The translation:

Horse for half a day

Hay for the horse

A-shoeing of him

And a-fetching of him again

Water mill. You can see this bill, and a few other treasures, at Letheringsett water mill, open all year Tues-Fri 0900-1300, 1400-1700, Sat 0900-1300, Sun 1400-1700.

The Domesday Book mentions 'Leringaseta,' and records of 1384 tell of John de Keyly and William de Gatele buying 48 acres of land *and a watermill*. By 1720 John Brereton owned the mill, the house which was to become Letheringsett Hall, and a brewery. Within the next few years the mill burned down, but was rebuilt by 1754. The next owner agreed with upstream landowners the depth of the millpond – a plaque by the weir reads *This water mark setled in the year 1765.* Fire destroyed the new mill in 1800, but it was working again in two years. Then in 1945 a Ruston & Hornsby diesel engine began driving the millstones, but as the public now wanted powder-fine white flour, the mill closed.

Restoration began in 1982, with the original water-wheel being adapted to work undershot or breastshot (i.e. at axle level), and now Letheringsett Mill is again in business, claiming to be the county's only working water-mill, its four sets of stones producing 2.5 tons of flour a week, mostly sold on the premises for animal and pet food.

Visit. You can tour the mill's working floors for 75p, or £1.50 on a demonstration day (Tues, Thur, Sun, bank hol, 1400-1630). The top floor was the last to be restored, using 10,500ft (3,200m) of plank from 200 oaks blown down in the gale of 16 October 1987.

Letheringsett Church. The round tower of St Andrew's church was built just after the Domesday census, but it is pure Saxon (pre-Conquest) in style, the windows being 15th-cent additions. In 1236 a local man gave land to **Binham Priory** which, in return, built the rest of the church. A Thomas Bacon was rector a few years later, but in 1308 the Prior of Binham began appointing priests, which continued until 1422. Then in 1458 John Heydon of Baconsthorpe began a century of Heydon patronage.

In 1786 John Burrell II, son-in-law of Mr Holmes, the head of Gresham's school, was appointed rector; a keen student of insects, he sold much of the Letheringsett estate to William Hardy who built a brewery – but had it any connection with the brewery opposite the water-mill? Hardy also planted many trees in the Glaven valley or, as his epitaph puts it, *he clothed these once-barren hills with foliage.*

The last person to be patron, before Keble College, Oxford, took over for the 1945 investiture, was Sir Alfred **Joddrell** of Bayfield, the man who built the tiny church at Glandford.

Johnson Jex. Look at the first tombstone on the right as you enter the churchyard. The 17-line epitaph is crumbling badly yet it still manages to praise the local blacksmith Johnson Jex who taught himself the art of watchmaking, which involved learning French unaided in order to read a book on the subject. He made every clockmaker's tool he needed, and he even engraved this verse inside a watch he made:

> I, Johnson Jex, a blacksmith bred,
> With some strange crankums in my head
> And tools on which I could depend
> By me invented. For a friend
> This time-piece made from end to end.
> If this your mind it should perplex
> Behold my name, 'tis Johnson Jex.

Some of Jex's watches and tools are in the Castle Museum, Norwich.

BAYFIELD. North of Letheringsett is the tiny village of Bayfield, represented mainly by the Hall, and by the church which was already in ruins by the 18th cent – if we can believe the pictures of Michael 'Angelo' Rooker, ARA, a scene painter at the Haymarket Theatre, London. In fact, the church was abandoned in 1927 when its last rector died, and it's now an ivy-clad skeleton. The last patron? None other than Sir Alfred Joddrell.

FELBRIGG HALL

The Felbrigg family created the estate and built the first Felbrigg Hall, but the beautiful country mansion that you see today is the work of the Windham family and was begun in 1620. William Windham I enhanced the property by planting the chestnuts in the 600-acre (240-ha) park, but it was William Windham II, returning from the Grand Tour in 1741, who did most for the hall. It was he who put the mid-18th cent touch to the interior and extended the main structure to hold the paintings collected on his tour: they are still at the hall and are a major feature. It was he who brought in the gilt mirrors, the furniture, and the damask hangings which now adorn the main rooms.

Finally, William Windham III, 'Weathercock' Windham, a politician who knew which way the political wind blew, added the final touches. 'Mad' Windham went bankrupt in 1863 and had to sell Felbrigg, the local merchant John Ketton being the lucky buyer. His grandson gave the hall to the National Trust in 1970 and it's now open late Mar-late Oct, daily ex Tues, Fri, 1330-1730 for around £4.30; gardens only, above dates, 1100-1730, around £1.60; 0263.75444.

The hall. Felbrigg Hall was enlarged in 1674-'87 and 1750, and is mainly in Jacobean style, with some excellent stucco plasterwork. The imposing south front, framed by three heavy chimney stacks, is probably the most memorable exterior feature as it has the words GLORIA DEO IN EXCELSIS set in the stonework of the parapet.

The hall has a restaurant open every day in season, a shop trading from 1200 on open days, with both opening (times as above) late Oct to Xmas. The park is open daily, dawn to dusk, thus allowing access to Felbrigg's **Church of St Margaret,** with its impressive tower and its monuments to the Felbrigg and Windham families, including the rarety of Felbrigg brasses of 1351 and 1380 in Norman French. There's some sculpting by Grinling Gibbons, too.

SOME CHURCHES

Travelling south from Felbrigg, a scattering of churches attracts one's attention – but first there's Andrew and Joanna Young's **Pottery** at Lower Gresham, south-west of Felbrigg Hall, specialising in traditional earthenware. The Youngs' work is known in several countries, and is represented in the Victoria & Albert Museum, London. Open year round 0900-1700, ✆0263.77548.

The churches begin with Ancient St Mary the Virgin's at **Roughton,** which has a short round tower, but the place is usually locked. **Thurgarton's** thatched All Saints' had a Saxon tower until its collapse in 1882, leaving the 13th cent west windows as the oldest parts. St Mary's at **Aldborough** still retains Saxon puddingstone masonry in the nave, but the place was heavily restored in 1847 and there's no tower here, either. **Thwaite's** round tower at All Saints' is not Saxon as it dates from 1275, but part of the north wall is pre-Conquest. St Ethelbert's at **Alby** has Saxon remains in its north wall, but its main interests are the priest's door into the chancel and the rood stairs.

Alby Crafts. You mustn't go through Alby without calling at the craft centre by the crossroads on the A140. Proprietor Valerie Alston (✆0263.761590) has restored some farm buildings to hold a furniture workshop, a watercolour artist, a couple who knit Shetland and Fair Isle wool, two portrait artists, a couple who work in porcelain, a worker in glass, and a photographer. There's also Lesley Thomas's **Lace Museum** and George Dennis's **Bottle Museum,** claimed to be unique in Britain and with 2,000 bottles on display. The centre is open Tues-Sun Mar-Dec 1000-1700.

You enter Our Lady and St Margaret's church at **Calthorpe** by the north-facing Devil's door, as the road is on that side. There's a touch of humour in a corbel showing one woman with her mouth open and another wearing a gag: was she the local gossip before and after punishment?

Erpingham's large Church of St Mary has a tall and imposing tower. The font came from St Benedict's in Norwich, a victim of World War

The deserted village of Godwick: remains of the church tower, kept as a folly, and a sheep trough.

Two, and shows saints Benedict, Peter, Jerome – and Faith, who was supposed to have been roasted alive on the gridiron she carries. Probably the most impressive sight is the brass to Sir John de Erpingham who died in 1370 and whose son Thomas built the imposing Erpingham Gate at Norwich Cathedral. There's grim humour in a corbel here, showing a man with his tongue extended: was he guilty of slander? If so, the medieval punishment is recalled in the grim jingle, *Tell tale tit, your tongue shall be slit.* Ugh!

St Lawrence's Church at **Ingworth** lost its Saxon round tower in 1822, so the stump is thatched to match the rest of the roof. The church was dilapidated in 1895 but restoration has left the box pews built in 1730, some of the oldest in the country.

Black Sheep. There's a Black Sheep wool shop opposite the church – but see more details in Aylsham.

WOLTERTON HALL

Wolterton Hall, west of Calthorpe, was built for Horace Walpole, youngest brother of Sir Robert Walpole, between 1727 and 1741. It was abandoned in 1858 in favour of **Mannington Hall,** two miles (3km) west, and was badly damaged by fire in 1952. Following the death of the owner, Lord Walpole, in 1989, the heir to the title has begun major restoration with the aim of reopening Wolterton. At the moment guided tours to parts of the house are available on prior application, although the gardens opened in 1991 with a programme of activities.

Mannington and Wolterton gardens are open Sun Apr-Oct, Wed-Fri May-Aug, 1100-1700 for £2, with a range of activities planned. Information on both, ✆0263.874175.

Birds of prey. Wolterton Hall is home to the **Hawk and Owl Trust,** a charity active in the conservation of these birds, but not the rescue of injured specimens; it's open from Easter. The **East Anglian Falconry Centre** at The Goat Inn, Skeyton, four miles east of Aylsham, *does* take in injured hawks and owls, and usually has more than 100 raptors, many of which are tame enough to handle. The centre is open daily, Apr-Oct 1000-1600, Nov-Mar, 1000-dusk, with flying displays every hour; ✆0692.69600.

AYLSHAM

Aylsham is a small market town with a cluster of interesting properties around the market place, notably the Black Boy Inn in Queen Anne style. Nearby, the Manor House dates from 1608, Old Hall from 1689, and The Knoll around 1700. The Buttlands, now a town-centre car park, is where townsmen were legally required to practice archery on Sundays until the 18th cent; archers' targets are known as 'butts.'

The first recorded mention of the town was around the Norman Conquest of 1066, when the priest was a Saxon known as Brithric. From 1087, under William II, Battle Abbey in Sussex appointed the priest, and took 10% of the local wheat harvest in return; this activity nationwide developed into the *tithe* which persisted in England until after World War Two – but Henry VIII ordered Aylsham's tithe to go to Canterbury after the dissolution of Battle Abbey.

Weaving. The town developed a wool- and linen-weaving industry, with records showing that in 1291 the Bishop of Hereford spent 18/– on four yards (4m) of cloth, and that in 1327 Edward II bought 3,500 ells of 'Aylleshamme.' Surely you remember that an 'ell' is 45in (1m 14) in England, 37in (94cm) in Scotland, 27in (68.6cm) in Flanders, and was originally the length of cloth you could wind around your elbow or 'ell-bow.'

John of Gaunt. John of Gaunt, youngest son of Edward III and father of Henry IV, became Squire of Aylsham in 1372, making it the main town in Norfolk of the Duchy of Lancaster and influencing design of the 'new' church, then being built; local legend claims that Edward III dictated the choice of site. When Gaunt died in 1399, Sir Thomas Erpingham became lord of Aylsham Manor for 15 years and influenced the churches here and in his native village.

St Michael's Church. The Victorians loved box pews, which look like early open-topped railway carriages. St Michael's pews are more conventional but with doors added to placate Victorian tastes. The columns supporting the nave roof do nothing for my tastes; I feel they lean outwards far too much but, officially, this was intentional. So ignore the columns and come to the church any Monday lunchtime May-Oct for a concert.

Robert Jannys, a wealthy Norwich merchant, bequeathed money in 1530 for what was probably the last chantry chapel to be licensed before the Reformation. The will added *tenn pounds by yeare for a priest's service to sing for me...and keep a free grammer schoole within Aylsham*. His merchant's mark has recently been added to a lady chapel window, but his school was lost in mergers.

Humphry Repton. Probably the best-known person to be buried here is Humphry Repton, the landscape gardener who was second only to 'Capability' Brown and who left his mark throughout the eastern counties. He died in 1818.

Under Queen Mary (1553-'58), when England again acknowledged the Pope as the head of the Church, John Bury, Vicar of Aylsham, condemned Thomas Hudson, a glove-maker, as a heretic, and had him burned at the stake in Norwich. Bury is mentioned in Fox's *Book of Martyrs* as *a very evil man...a great swearer, given to women, persecuting the gospel and compelling men to idolatry*. He was a veritable 'black sheep' in the clerical flock.

Black Sheep. The light grey Norfolk Horn was the sheep which gave East Anglia its woollen wealth, but Black Sheep Ltd, a knitwear factory in Penfold St, specialises in the fleece of the black Welsh Mountain sheep from its flock kept at Ingworth. The firm's owner, Mrs Clare Hoare, began in 1966 with six sheep which she got by swapping an old lawn mover; the flock now peaks at around 1,000. Open year round Tues-Sun, 0900-1730; ✆0263.733142.

BURE VALLEY RAILWAY. British Rail had removed all the track along the route between Aylsham and Hoveton, but enthusiasts of the Bure Valley Railway replaced it with 15in (38cm) gauge lines and opened for business on 11 July 1990, covering the nine miles (14.5km) through Brampton, Buxton and Coltishall, and meeting the BR main line at Wroxham Station – which is really in Hoveton. Steam and diesel trains run late Mar-Dec, peaking with a seven-every-day service in Aug; full details in *Discover Norwich and the Broads*, or ✆0263.733858; ♿ passengers are carried by arrangement.

BLICKLING HALL

You must not visit Aylsham without calling in at Blickling Hall, ranking in my opinion equal top with Houghton and Holkham as the most historically and architecturally interesting stately home in Norfolk, and now the regional headquarters for the National Trust, its owner.

Anne Boleyn. Blickling is best known as the birthplace of Anne Boleyn, yet there is no proof that Anne was born on this site: as the event happened in 1507 it certainly was not in *this* house which was begun in 1616.

King Harold owned the Blickling lands until his death at the Battle of Hastings in 1066. William the Conqueror gave Blickling to Herbert de Losinga, Bishop of Norwich, from whom it passed to the Fastolf family.

Execution. Sir Geoffrey's descendant Thomas, Earl of Wiltshire, was the father of Anne and George Boleyn (Viscount Rochford). Anne was too beautiful for her own good, distracting Henry VIII's eye even while he was married to Catherine of Aragon. Anne married the king on 14 November 1532 according to one source, and 25 January 1533 according to another, yet Henry's first marriage was not annulled until May 1533. Anne gave birth to the future Queen Elizabeth I on 7 September 1533, and lost her head on the block on 19 May, 1536, two days after her brother George was executed. This line of the Boleyn family died with George, but the name survives as 'Bullen.'

Ghosts. Anne's heart was probably buried in Erwarton Church near Ipswich, and for ages her ghost, carrying its severed head under its arm, was supposed to come to Blickling Hall in a coach drawn by four headless horses.

Modern Blickling. Sir Henry Hobart, Lord Chief Justice, began rebuilding the hall in 1616, his son completing the work. The hall passed to the Marquesses of Lothian, the 11th Marquess being Britain's ambassador to the USA when he died in 1940, leaving the hall

The Norfolk Shire Horse Centre at West Runton gives demonstrations of these beautiful animals working the land.

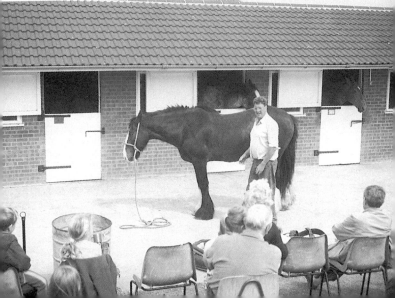

and the 4,500-acre (1,800-ha) estate to the National Trust. The hall is **open** Apr-Oct daily ex Mon, Thur, 1300-1700; gardens as above but from 1200; parkland year round, dawn to dusk; admission to hall and gardens £4.90; in addition there are special events; for details ℡0263.733084.

See the hall for yourself, and marvel: at the Long Gallery, which the 2nd Earl of Buckinghamshire built to hold a massive tapestry of Peter the Great of Russia at the Battle of Poltava; at the splendid library begun in the 18th cent; at George II's bedhangings in the state bedroom; outside, see the formal gardens in part designed by Humphry Repton.

St Andrew's Church. Blickling's stubby-towered church is mostly 15th cent but, being where it is, has numerous memorials and brasses. "Here lies Nicholas de Dagworth, Knight, formerly Lord of Blickling" and the builder of the first hall; he died in 1401. A brass commemorates Anna Boleyn – but this Anna died in 1479 in her fourth year. Several other Boleyns are remembered, but if you want an insight into 15th-cent life, look at the brass to Roger and Cecily Felthorp, shown with their 10 sons and 6 daughters. Interesting – but such brasses and statues are found elsewhere, and the family was not excessively large.

CAWSTON. Four miles (6.5km) south-west of Aylsham is Cawston, a village with an unusual story. Early Britons were living here at least 1,200 years BC, proved by the discovery of a burial urn. The Romans probably stayed awhile in the area, losing some of their coins which have since been found. The Danes certainly put down roots here; so did the Saxons. King Harold owned this manor as well as Blickling's, and so it passed direct to William I. William II's Domesday survey mentions the farming community here, surrounded by a vast forest.

Eventually the **Earls of Suffolk** took control of the manor, and it was Michael de la Pole, one of those earls, who was responsible for beginning **St Agnes's Church** in 1350, although the building is so large that it understandably took 150 years to finish. The tower is enormous, fit for a cathedral, and it's built of stone shipped from Normandy and presumably hauled overland from the Wensum or the Bure; the roof of the nave is as tall as a four-storey house.

The parish fortunes went into decline soon after the church was finished, and the stained glass windows were sold. Remains of pits to the north of the church held the bodies of plague victims, and were last used in 1832 after an outbreak of cholera: the north of the church was also where the excommunicated of any parish were buried.

St Agnes. In the 3rd-cent Roman Empire, being a Christian was punishable with death. The son of a Roman civil servant courted Agnes, the daughter of a noble family, but she spurned him, stating she would marry Christ. She was arrested, burned at the stake, and her head was chopped off into the fire. As her name is similar to the Latin *agnus,* 'lamb,' a lamb is shown in Cawston Church's east window and on the roof.

NORTH WALSHAM

The Saxons built the first church in North Walsham. It was enlarged in 1275, then rebuilt from ground level around 1330. Work stopped in 1348 when the Black Death killed 80% of the population in several villages in the eastern counties. Work stopped again in 1361 and '69 for the same reasons and, when it was resumed, the loss of skilled masons forced a much simpler design to be adopted on the side windows, still apparent more than six centuries later.

Peasants' Revolt. There were delays yet again in 1381 when John (or was it Geoffrey?) Litester of Worstead (or was it Felmingham?) emerged as the local leader of the Peasants' Revolt, supporting Wat Tyler of Wymondham. After losing a battle outside the town – a cross is supposed to mark the spot – Litester sought sanctuary with his followers in North Walsham church, but Hugh Despenser, Bishop of Norwich, abused the sanctuary principle and had them all slaughtered. Soon after, the church was dedicated to St Mary the Virgin, changing to St Nicholas after the Reformation.

Church. The church's original tower was Saxon, but *square,* as the builders used local ironstone for the corners. A later and larger tower, also square, was built beside this original, almost swallowing it, and at the height of its glory the tower reached 147ft (45m) tall, second only to that at Cromer, but when you consider the spire on top of *that,* it reached 170ft (52m), second only in the county to Norwich cathedral spire.

During the Ascension Day Fayre on 15 May 1724, the five bells were rung for hours: the next day the tower and steeple collapsed. More stone fell in 1835, and a gale of 1836 did further damage, resulting in a 'temporary' repair and a tower just 88ft (27m) tall. The stump of the Saxon tower now holds the heating system.

Inside the nave you will find a very good example of a telescopic font cover and, 15ft (5m) up the wall in the north-west corner, a blocked doorway to the priest's chamber of Saxon times. Sir William Paston ordered his own tomb in 1607, to show *a man in armour, restinge vpon his arme, of fiue foot and a halfe longe in alabaster,* which is still quite impressive. The day after Sir William was buried here, in 1610, his wife's body was exhumed from Paston Church and reburied beside him. This same William Paston founded the town's Paston School, which counted Horatio Nelson among its pupils. The elegant south porch has the arms of John of Gaunt, who held this parish with that of Aylsham, and others.

The town. Legend claims that the smart **market cross** was built between 1550 and 1554, but 1558 seems a more likely date. It was badly damaged in the **fire** which raged through town on 25 June 1600, destroying most of the timber-framed houses. Oh – market day is Thursday.

Cat Pottery. If you are looking for something different, go to the Cat Pottery and Railway Junkyard in Grammar School Rd; it's opposite the Black Cat Garage yet has no connection. Ken and Jenny Allen have taken a tinsmith's workshop and converted it into a factory for making pottery cats and dogs of all sizes and shapes imaginable; they even make the glass eyes.

Son Nick began collecting the railway memorabilia which is now scattered around the place – he calls it the 'junkyard' – but it's there only for looking at: he won't sell any. Open Mon-Fri 0900-1700, plus Sat various hours; ✆0692.402962.

WORSTEAD

Many cloths take their name of the place where they were first woven. Calico comes from Calicut, now Calcutta, and damask from Damascus, but cashmere probably takes its name from 'kerseymere,' named from the Suffolk village of Kersey, rather than from Kashmir. Worsted, however – spelled without an 'A' – certainly originated in Worstead.

The present village is just a collection of pleasant houses around a large market square, but each one has a story. With your back to the church you are facing St Andrew's Cottage, where steps in the front garden go down to a cellar. Legend fancifully claims this as the entrance to a smugglers' tunnel that went to Happisburgh or, slightly more believable, to the now-vanished St Andrew's Church. Parish records have the will of Agnes Watts, drawn up in 1321 and leaving £25 to pay for candles to be burned in perpetuity in the church.

On your left is **Geoffrey the Dyer's House,** named from Geoffrey Litester (North Walsham Church calls him 'John') who led the local Peasants' Revolt against the Poll Tax. But as Litester never lived here, he could possibly have been a Felmingham man; the so-called Dyer's House was really a row of weavers' cottages and might have been a merchant's house at some time. The owner runs the Anna Sewell Restaurant in Great Yarmouth and offers B&B here at Worstead.

St Mary's Church. Opposite, facing the church, is the old Manor House; then you come to the church itself, begun in 1379 and large enough to hold the entire population several times over, a testimony to the power and wealth that the woollen industry generated in the Middle Ages.

The tower is 109ft (33m) tall, and the nave has some impressively strong flying buttresses; as a result, the columns supporting the roof are dead upright. Your first impression will be of the size of the nave, then you will notice the box pews and the hammerbeam roof; the church's own guide gives a detailed description of the building's finer points, such as the priest's chamber which was built over the vestry in 1450.

St Mary's Guild of Weavers, Spinners and Dyers perpetuates the village's golden age by maintaining a **museum** inside the church, showing samples of wool from several breeds of sheep, their possible faults, and the manufacture of worsted cloth, a fine material from long-staple wool. The guild keeps a dozen or so old-style looms in the nave, and practises on them so that the ancient skills are kept alive.

Worstead is normally a quiet village, but come during the late-July festival and you'll find music and dance, vintage cars and BMX bikes.

SOME MORE CHURCHES

Moving north from North Walsham, the thatched Church of St Nicholas at **Swafield** shows the saint with his three gold balls or bags, thereby linking Santa Claus with the Turkish saint and the pawn-broker. **Trunch's** Church of St Botolph has a tower 95ft (29m) tall, but its main attractions are the font canopy, one of four of its kind in the country, and the chancel screen, carved in 1502; this survived the Puritanic purge of 1643 only because the chancel was used as the school room – you can still see initials scratched in the walls. **Knapton** has one of England's best double-hammerbeam roofs, made in 1503-'04 from Irish oak, spanning 30ft 6in (9m 30) and almost as good as new five centuries later. Legend claims that the roof was made in some remote area for some unknown church, but found its way to Knapton as spoils from a shipwreck. The parish has some impressive names among its lords of the manor, including William de Warrenne; John de Vere, Earl of Oxford; John Nevill, Lord Latimer; and Thomas Cecil, Earl of Exeter.

West, at **Antingham,** the ruins of the 12th-cent St Margaret's church stand beside the still-used Church of St Mary, with the parish boundary running between them. The brass to Richard Calthorpe, who died in 1562, shows him with his 19 children.

Up the A149, **Thorpe Market** has a towerless church built in 1795-'96 in 'churchwarden's Gothick' style, but **Southrepps** has a traditional church in St James's, with a tower 114ft (34.5m) high. It has a long nave and chancel and, before 1791 when it lost its north and south aisles, it was as big as a cathedral. **Trimingham,** to the north, has its Church of St John the Baptist's Head, a bizarre dedication that owes its origins to the legend that the saint's severed head was actually in the church. The belief was so strong that people came here on pilgrimage. The tower is squat and well buttressed outside, and even in the nave.

William de Warrenne was lord of the manor of **Gimingham** as well as founder of the Cluniac Priory at Lewes, Sussex, in 1077, so it's no surprise to learn that All Saints' Church had its preachers appointed by the prior. **John of Gaunt** was a later squire and while the site of his manor is unknown, the village still has a house called John of Gaunt's Hall.

MUNDESLEY

William Cowper spent his last years – 1795-1800 – alternating between his cousin's house in High St, Mundesley, and East Dereham. Cowper, best known for his poem **John Gilpin,** was suffering from depression and eventually left Mundesley because he didn't like the east wind.

The village, pronounced *Munzly*, was mentioned in the Domesday survey as Muleslai, and made its living by fishing despite the absence of a harbour. The railway's arrival in 1898 turned Mundesley into a minor holiday resort, which it still is, despite the railway's departure in 1964. The Royal Hotel, built in the late 17th cent, claims that Horatio Nelson was a guest while he studied at North Walsham.

Lifeboat. Understandably, the village has always turned its face towards the sea. It had a lifeboat from 1811 to 1895, with William Withers its coxwain from 1841 to 1881. Under Withers's command the boat saved six men from the *George* on 17 November 1868, then went out again the next day and saved the entire crew of the *Restless*. In the 19th cent, small coastal vessels would beach themselves on the ebb tide near the lifeboat slipway, discharge their cargo of coal into horse-drawn carts, load up with grain, and get away on the next flood tide.

The village sits on a vein of clay which provided the material for most of its bricks, but the last trace of the industry is the office at the Kiln Cliffs Caravan Park: it's an old kiln.

All Saints' Church, a towerless 20th-cent renovation of a 14th-cent ruin, had two notorious rectors in Tudor times; John Russell was a part-time poacher, and James Matchett was a minor criminal who was frequently in court.

Stow Mill. South of the village is Stow Mill, built in 1827 and abandoned in the 1930s. Teacher Mike Newton bought it in 1971 and has done most of the restoration including rebuilding the sails, brought down by a gale in September 1978. The mill is open daily, usually unattended, so you're honour-bound to make a 30p donation, or 80p if you climb to the top.

Mundesley today. The village offers quiet holidays and is a good base for seeing the neighbourhood. The **beach** is moderately wide, with sand at the top and some shingle lower; accommodation ranges from smart hotel to caravan site. **Tourist office,** Station Rd, ✆0263.721070. The annual 'Bonanza' is on Spring Bank Holiday.

PASTON and BACTON

The tiny village of Paston owes its fame to members of the Paston family who not only wrote to prominent and not-so-prominent people between 1422 and 1509, but *who got the letters back and kept them*. The Paston Letters are therefore almost the earliest known text written in English, and are a good first-hand account of life in the reigns of Henry VI, Edward IV and V, Richard II and Henry VII, and spanning the Civil Wars.

The Paston Letters. The Pastons kept the letters as a family record, but when the last of the line, William Paston, Earl of Yarmouth, died in 1732, they were sold. A chemist in Diss had them in 1774, selling them to John Fenn of East Dereham who published 155 of them, with related documents, in 1787: he cleared the first edition within a week. His fifth volume was ready when he died in 1794 having edited 485 documents.

This was penned in 1425, the þ being an early form of *th* as in 'the, that:'

> To my well beloued John Staynford of Furnyvales Inne.
>
> To enquerre and wyte whether þe stoon may be sawed or nought, and whether it wille chippe or chynne or affraye with frost of weder or water.
>
> Al-so þat euery pece of þe stoon be iij foote longe and þat xv tunne tygh...[lost]...of þe stoon be euery weel bedded in-to þe walle and a foote thikke þat it ryse in heighte a foote in þe walle..

Difficult, isn't it? In 1464 the first John Paston petitioned Edward IV to urge him to make certain appointments to the church:

> To the Kyng owre sovereyn Lord
>
> Please it yowre Highnes to graunte vn-to yowre humble seruant John Paston the older, squier, yowr gracious lettres patentz of licence to fownde, stabilysh, and endewe in the gret mancion of Castre be Mekyll Yermowth [Caister by Great Yarmouth; *muckle* is a dialect word still in use, meaning 'much' or 'great'] in Norffolk, that late was John Fastolffes, knyght, cosyn to yowre seyd besecher, a colage of vij prystes...

This was the John Paston who owned Gresham Castle, and whose wife was besieged there when Paston went away on business. The family began in a fairly humble manner, the oldest preserved document being an indenture of 1341 for Clement de Paston and his son William. A later Clement bequeathed a few shillings each to the churches at Paston, Trunch and Mundesley, in 1419, with 6/8d to Bromholm Priory.

This Clement put his son William to school, often borrowing to pay for the education. William studied law, qualified as a Justice (judge), and with these moneymaking skills gradually built up the family estates, buying land in Paston and Bacton, then later in Snailwell (Cambs), Gresham, and adding lands at Stanstead (Suffolk) by marriage. The Pastons grew in influence and importance but had passed their prime by the time the last of them died.

St Margaret's Church. The 14th-cent thatched church has numerous memorials and tombs to members of the Paston family, but several can no longer be identified individually as they were moved to make way for the imposing tombs of Katherine Paston and, later, her husband Edmund. The man who made the first one wrote in his diary that he was *pay'd for it £340,* a sum which, in 1628 values, would take the average farmhand around five lifetimes to earn. The inscription reads:

> The vertvovs...lady Dame Katherine Paston daughter
> vnto...Sr Thomas Knevitt...
>> Not that fhee nedeth monument of ftone
>> for her weel gotten fame to reft vppon
>> But this was reard to teftifie that fhee
>> lives in their loves...

A brass in the sanctuary recalls Erasmus Paston, father of the founder of Paston School in North Walsham, and opposite the main door is a medieval mural of St Christopher, discovered in 1922. He is carrying the baby Jesus, who has six toes on one foot.

The large **Paston Barn,** in a field west of the church, was built in 1581 and is still in very good order. If you ask around you might be allowed inside but, in view of its size, condition and history, I'm surprised its tourist potential hasn't been exploited.

Bacton Gas Terminal. Five hundred metres east of the medieval barn we are plunged into the late 20th century with the Bacton Gas Terminal, which is in the parish of Paston. The story of North Sea gas began in 1959 when the Dutch struck methane two miles (3km) down, trapped beneath a vertical mile of rock salt. Britain's first gas strike was confirmed in 1965 in the West Sole field, which is piped ashore in Holderness. Shell and Esso found the biggest gas field, the Leman Bank, in 1966, soon followed by Indefatigable, Hewett, Dottie Deborah and others.

When it was obvious the gas would be piped ashore in Norfolk, work began on a 200-acre (80-ha) site in Paston parish to receive the fuel at the rate of 4,000,000,000cu ft (115,000,000cu m) a day, for cleaning and onward transmission to customers across most of the country. The terminal is so well designed and landscaped that only two derricks and a cluster of roofs are visible; it is not open to the

North Walsham's Market Cross was badly damaged in the fire of 1600.

public.

Bromholm Priory. South of Bacton village are the remains of Bromholm Priory which, despite their history, are scarcely worth seeing.

HAPPISBURGH

The Domesday survey called this community Hapesburgh, but its name is now pronounced *Hayz-br*. William the Conqueror gave the manor to Roger Bigod of the family which was soon to rise to prominence. But when the head of William I's household, **William d'Albini** married Bigod's daughter Maud, he received Happisburgh as a wedding present.

Wymondham Abbey. D'Albini built Castle Rising, and founded a priory which was to become the great Wymondham Abbey, and he gave Happisburgh to the abbey's first prior.

Dangerous coast. In the 14th cent, Happisburgh's Norman church was demolished to make way for the present structure, its tower to serve as a landmark for 500 years along a particularly dangerous stretch of coast, for the treacherous Happisburgh Sands are not far offshore.

Daniel Defoe, author of *Robinson Crusoe*, commented in 1724 on the number of ships' timbers used in barns and other buildings in the neighbourhood. If he could return today he would learn that, despite the tower being a navigational aid, the churchyard holds the bodies of

Bishop Bonner's Cottage Museum by East Dereham parish church

hundreds of shipwreck victims, including a mass grave for 119 seamen from HMS *Invincible*, wrecked on the sands on 13 March 1801.

Lighthouses. Two lighthouses were already on station at Happisburgh when the warship went aground; one was demolished late in the 19th cent. When Trinity House announced in June 1988 that it wanted to decommission the remaining light, local people objected. Within a month the Happisburgh Lighthouse Trust was formed, but it soon learned that the law forbids anybody but Trinity House from operating a lighthouse. The answer was obvious: the law must be changed. The NatWest Bank paid the £15,000 that was needed to get the Bill through Parliament and in August 1990 Trinity House leased the working lighthouse to the trust, which now runs it as Britain's only private working light. It's *not* open to the public.

Church. That other landmark, the church tower, stands on a hilltop overlooking the North Sea. To make it distinctive the villagers had mounted a large crucifix on the top. It fell in 1818 and was replaced. In 1822 lightning struck the second one, damaged the tower, and set the nave roof on fire, forcing services to be held in the chancel until restoration was completed in 1864.

So let us end with the happier story about the Rev Thomas Lloyd who, in 1793 noting the few baptisms in the village, suspected that the parents couldn't pay for the customary party that should follow. He offered a mass baptism with a free feast after it – and 170 people came.

130

7: SWAFFHAM and DEREHAM

High Norfolk

THE ANCIENT MARKET TOWNS of Swaffham and East Dereham (West Dereham is near Downham Market) grew in importance as they were on the coaching route between Lynn and Norwich, now the A47. But, as Norfolk never entered the Industrial Revolution, neither town has expanded to another Birmingham or Bradford – and therein lies their charm, as we shall see in this necessarily brief glimpse.

SWAFFHAM

As you enter Swaffham Market Place from the west, you cannot fail to see the town sign, showing the Swaffham Pedlar, 'who by a dream did find great fortune.'

The legend claims that the pedlar, John Chapman, dreamed that if he went to London Bridge he would meet a man who would make his fortune. When he reached the bridge a man asked him why he was loitering, so Chapman told of his dream. The Londoner scoffed, saying that if *he* paid attention to dreams he would have gone to Swaffham and dug in the garden of a man called Chapman.

The pedlar went home and unearthed a pot full of gold coins, with another pot, twice as big, hidden beneath it.

The real Chapman. The truth is that John Chapman was a merchant and churchwarden, who helped finance the building of the parish church around 1460; he is seen in the carvings on the front pew-ends, in the clergy stalls in the chancel, and his dog sits on the gable of the south porch. But did he finance the building from trading, or from some pot of gold?

Cromwell connection. The south transept has a memorial of 1590 to Catherine Steward, whose claim to fame is that she was Oliver Cromwell's maternal grandmother.

DEREHAM

East Dereham's legends are about the town's creator, Withburga, youngest daughter of King Anna, who established a convent here in

654. Withburga found she was running short of food, so the Virgin Mary sent two wild deer each day for Withburga to milk, and so save her community. When death called, she was buried in a tomb over which a chapel was built, and for several centuries this tomb attracted pilgrims to Dereham.

Withburga's sister Ethelreda had inherited the Isle of Ely and had begun her own convent there, but in 974 the monks at Ely decided that Saint Withburga's remains should rest there, not in Dereham. They threw a banquet in Dereham then under cover of night stole the body: another legend claims that although three centuries had passed the corpse was in perfect condition.

Holy spring. The Virgin Mary compensated the people of Dereham for their loss by making a spring of clear water flow from the open tomb, which brought pilgrims in increasing numbers even though marauding Vikings had destroyed the convent around 870.

St Withburga's spring dried up in the 18th cent, but her open tomb is still visible amid the ruins of the chapel to the west of St Nicholas's Church. St Nicholas? Why wasn't it dedicated to St Withburga?

The church's large tower, built in 1530, stands separate from the main building as the original tower is still there, but not sturdy enough to hold all the eight bells. This later tower was used as an overnight prison for French trooper Jean de Narde during the Napoleonic wars. Narde escaped, was shot, and is buried near St Withburga's ruined chapel. And the church tower is now a **tourist office,** open daily Apr-Sep, 1300-1600.

Bishop Bonner. Almost at the entrance to the churchyard is **Bishop Bonner's Cottage Museum,** set in one of the most intriguing small buildings in East Anglia. Edward Bonner was the local rector from 1534 to '38 before becoming Bishop of London. The three cottages, knocked into one, have the date MDII (1502) in the pargeting (plasterwork), but there is no known link between them and Bonner, nor is anything known of the cottages before this century.

Part of the building became a museum in 1963, the remainder coming into use in 1968 to create the present museum of local history, including a section on the town's literary men, but the building itself is the main exhibit, with its three staircases and a passage so narrow that one must walk sideways. It's open May-Sep Tues-Sat 1430-1700, donations welcomed.

Borrow and Cowper. William Cowper, who didn't like the east winds at Mundesley, moved to a house on Dereham Market Place, the site now occupied by the Congregational Church, and spent his last four miserable years here; he was buried in St Nicholas's churchyard in 1800.

By contrast, George Borrow's parents were married in the church, and Borrow was brought up in the town, but his mother went to

Dumpling Green, a mile south, for the birth in 1803. Borrow is best known for his *Lavengro*, published in 1851.

GRESSENHALL MUSEUM

In 1774 the authorities built an enormous workhouse for 700 luckless people from the Dereham area. Today it is the Gressenhall Museum, which the *Independent* has listed as one of the country's top 50 museums. It's on the B1146, two miles (3km) north-east of town, open Easter-Oct Tues-Sat (plus bank hols) 1000-1700, Sun 1400-1730, for around £2; ✆0362.860563.

The museum holds a wide range of photos and artefacts showing rural life in the past 150 years, with other sections recalling the tools of now-defunct trades. The largest display is, understandably, of farm implements including ploughs, wagons, and a range of tools that sprang from Jethro Tull's invention of the seed drill: mechanical weeders, turnip thinners, and corn drills. One threshing machine has particular interest as it was made by William Foster of Lincoln, who built the first Army tank.

Here are the re-creations of the seedsman's shop, the dairy, the forge, the weaver's shop, the saddlery, and even the country cottage. And to complete the display of local life there's a *mawkin* – that's a Norfolk dialect word, probably a scathing corruption of the American *Mohican*, because it means 'scarecrow.'

Some of the splendid array of exhibits in the Gressenhall Museum near East Dereham.

8: WHEN THE SUN GOES DOWN

Accommodation in north Norfolk

THIS LIST OF ACCOMMODATION is compiled from information supplied by the North Norfolk and West Norfolk district councils, the North Norfolk Hotel and Guest House Association, and the Youth Hostels Association; it includes few accommodations of less than four bedrooms.

Symbols. The symbols used are: ✆ phone number of premises, ⇝ number of bedrooms, ✿ building is of historic interest, ✕ restaurant, ♀ licensed to serve alcohol, ⅙ some services for disabled people, ⇚ number of touring caravan sites and ▲ of camp sites. The absence of a symbol may mean a lack of information, not lack of service.

HOTELS, GUEST HOUSES, B&B

AYLSHAM:
Buckinghamshire Arms, Blickling, ✆0263.733471, ⇝3, ✿ ✕ ♀.

BACTON:
Seacroft, Beach Rd, ✆0692.650302, ⇝7.

BRANCASTER:
Briarfields, Main St, Titchwell, ✆0485.210742, ⇝12, ✕. St Mary's House, London St, ✆0485.210774, ⇝3. Titchwell Manor, ✆0485.210221, ⇝16, ✕.

The BURNHAMS:
Domville Guest Ho, Glebe La, Overy Staithe, ✆0328.738298, ⇝7. Hoste Arms, B. Market, ✆0328.738257, ⇝12, ✿ ✕ ♀.

CLEY:
Flintstones, Wiveton, ✆0263.740337, ⇝5.

CROMER hotels:
Anglia Court, 6 Runton Rd, ✆0263.512443, ⇝28, ✕ ♀. Church Barn, Church St, Northrepps, ✆0263.78691, ⇝5, ✿ ✕ ♀. Cliftonville, 29 Runton Rd, ✆0263.512543, ⇝44, ✕ ♀. Dormy House, West Runton, ✆0263.75537, ⇝16, ✕. Mayfair, 27 Cabbell Rd, ✆0263.511681, ⇝9. Red Lion, Brook St, ✆0263.514964, ⇝12, ✕ ♀. Sandcliff, Runton Rd, ✆0263.512888, ⇝24, ✕ ♀. Virginia Court, Cliff Ave, ✆0263.512398, ⇝28, ✕ ♀. Westgate Lodge, 10 Macdonald Rd, ✆0263.512840, ⇝11, ✕ ♀.

CROMER other:

Bath House, The Promenade, ✆0263.514260, ⇚7. Beachcomber, 17 Macdonald Rd, ✆0263.513398, ⇚7. Birch House, 34 Cabbell Rd, ✆0263.512521, ⇚8. Brightside, 19 Macdonald Rd, ✆0263.513408, ⇚6. Cambridge House, Sea Front, ✆0263.512085, ⇚6. Chellow-Dene, 23 Macdonald Rd, ✆0263.513251, ⇚8. Danum House, 22 Pauls La, Overstrand, ✆0263.78327, ⇚4, ✿, Apr-Oct. Grove, 95 Overstrans Rd, ✆0263.512412, ⇚9, Apr-Oct. Knoll, 23 Alfred Rd, ✆0263.512753, ⇚5. Morden House, Cliff Ave, ✆0263.513396, ⇚7. Pleasaunce, Christian Holiday Centre, Overstrand, ✆0263.78212, ⇚33, ✿ ✗. White Horse, West St, ✆0263.512275, ⇚6.

DERSINGHAM:

Spring Cottage, 11 Fern Hill, ✆0485.541012, ⇚3. Westdene House, 60 Hunstanton Rd, ✆0485.540395, ⇚5, ✗ ⴲ. White House, 44 Hunstanton Rd, ✆0485.541895, ⇚4, ♿.

DOCKING:

Choseley Farmhouse, ✆0485.26331, ⇚2. Haddin, Ringstead Rd, ✆0485.518701, ⇚2. Helen's, North Farm Ho, Station Rd, ✆0485.8493, ⇚3. Holland House, Chequers St, ✆0485.518295, ⇚5.

FAKENHAM:

Lowfields Hotel, Hayes La, ✆0328.855432, ⇚12, ✗ ⴲ. Old Coach House, Thursford, ✆0328.878273, ✿.

Gt BIRCHAM:

King's Head, ✆0485.23265, ⇚5, ✗ ⴲ ♿.

GRIMSTON:

Congham Hall Country House, ✆0485.600250, ⇚14, ✗ ⴲ.

HAPPISBURGH:

Cliff House, Beach Rd, ✆0692.650775, ⇚4.

HEACHAM:

Holly House, 3 Broadway, ✆0485.72092, ⇚3. St Ann's, 53 Neville Rd, ✆0485.70021, ⇚8, ⴲ.

HOLT:

Glavenside, Letheringsett, ✆0263.713181, ⇚6. Lawns, Station Rd, ✆0263.713390, ⇚11.

HUNSTANTON: hotels

Burleigh, Cliff Tce, ✆0485.533080, ⇚11, ✗ ⴲ. Caley Hall, Old Hunstanton, ✆0485.533486, ⇚29, ✿ ✗ ⴲ ♿. Deepdene, 29 Avenue Rd, ✆0485.532460, ⇚9, ⴲ. Golden Lion, The Green, ✆0485.532688, ⇚31, ✗ ⴲ ♿. Le Strange Arms, Golf Course Rd, ✆0485.534411, ⇚38, ✗ ⴲ. Linksway, Golf Course Rd, ✆0485.532209, ⇚14, ✗ ⴲ. Lodge, Old Hunstanton Rd, ✆0485.532896, ⇚16, ✗ ⴲ ♿. Pinewood, 26 Northgate, ✆0485.533068, ⇚8, ✗ ⴲ. Shelbrooke, 9 Cliff Tce, ✆0485.532289, ⇚9, ⴲ. Sunningdale, 3 Avenue Rd, ✆0485.532562, ⇚11, ✗ ⴲ. Sutton House, 24 Northgate, ✆0485.532552, ⇚7, ✗ ⴲ. Wash and Tope, Le Strange Tce, ✆0485.532250, ⇚10, ✗ ⴲ.

HUNSTANTON: other

Ambleside, 50 Victoria Ave, ✆0485.534520, ⇚4, ♿. Caltofts, 15 Austin St, ✆0485.533759, ⇚6. Cambridge House, 32 Westgate, ✆0485.534552, ⇚8, ⴲ. Claremont, 35 Greevegate, ✆0485.533171, ⇚7, ⴲ. Ellinbrook House, 37 Avenue Rd, ✆0485.532022, ⇚6, ⴲ. Gate Lodge, 2 Westgate, ✆0485.533549, ⇚6, ⴲ ♿. Gemini Lodge, ✆0485.533902, ⇚6, ♿. Kew Cottage, 49 Crescent Rd, ✆0485.534205, ⇚4.

Pronounce it *duck* but spell it DUKW: a wartime amphibious vehicle still on duty at Hunstanton.

Kiama Cottage, 23 Austin St, ✆0485.533615, ⇌4. **Lakeside,** Waterworks Rd, ✆0485.533763, ⇌5, ✗ ⏛. **Nara House,** 9 Lincoln Sq, ✆0485.534290, ⇌4. **Newton,** 41 Victoria Ave, ✆0485.532756, ⇌5. **Northgate House,** 46 Northgate, ✆0485.533269, ⇌6. **Oceanview,** 66 Northgate, ✆0485.532364, ⇌5, ⏛. **Oriel Lodge,** 24 Homefields Rd, ✆0485.532368, ⇌5. **Peacock House,** 28 Park Rd, ✆0485.534040, ⇌10, ✗ ⏛ ♿. **Rosamaly,** 14 Glebe Ave, ✆0485.534187, ⇌5.

KING'S LYNN: hotels

Belgrave, 14 St John's Tce, ✆✆0553.772801, ⇌10, ✗ ⏛. **Butterfly,** Beveridge Way, ✆✆0553.771701, A10-A47 roundabout, Hardwick Narrows, ⇌48, ✗ ⏛ ♿. **Duke's Head,** Tuesday Market Pl, ✆✆0553.774996, ⇌72, ✗ ⏛ ♿. **Glendevon,** Railway Rd, ✆✆0553.773019, ⇌8, ✗ ⏛. **Globe,** Tuesday Market Pl, ✆✆0553.772617, ⇌40, ✗ ⏛. **Grange,** Willow Pk, South Wootton Lane, ✆✆0553.673777, ⇌10, ✗ ⏛. **Guanock,** Guanock Pl, South Gates, ✆✆0553.772959, ⇌17, ⏛. **Knight's Hill,** South Wootton, ✆✆0553.675566, ⇌58, ✗ ⏛ ♿. **Red Cat,** North Wootton, ✆✆0553.631224, ⇌7, ✗ ⏛. **Russett House,** 53 Goodwins Rd, ✆✆0553.773098, ⇌12, ✗ ⏛. **Stuart House,** 35 Goodwins Rd, ✆✆0553.772169, ⇌21, ✗ ⏛. **Tudor Rose,** St Nicholas St, ✆✆0553.762824, ⇌14, ✗ ⏛.

KING'S LYNN: other

Bank House, King's Staithe Sq, ✆✆0553.765087, ⇌4, ✗ ⏛. **Beeches,** 2 Guanock Tce, ✆✆0553.766577, ⇌7, ⏛. **Christa's,** 92 London Rd, ✆✆0553.772271, ⇌3. **Fairlight Lodge,** 79 Goodwins Rd, ✆✆0553.762234, ⇌6, ♿. **Gables,** 86 Tennyson Rd, ✆✆0553.768540, ⇌4. **Havana,** 117 Gaywood Rd, ✆✆0553.772331, ⇌7. **Maranatha,** 115 Gaywood Rd, ✆✆0553.774596, ⇌6, ✗ ⏛. **Oakview,** 107 Tennyson Rd, ✆✆0553.771180, ⇌3. **Rosedale,** 68 Goodwins Rd, ✆✆0553.764049, ⇌3, ♿. **61,** George Ave, ✆✆0553.774485, ⇌3. **St Helen's,** Saddlebow, ✆✆0553.617543, ⇌5. **Twinson Lee,** 109 Tennyson Rd, ✆✆0553.762900, ⇌3. **Windsor,** 35 London Rd, ✆✆0553.760164, ⏛.

MUNDESLEY:
Manor, ☎0263.720309, ⇌28, ✿ ✕ ☲. Overcliff Lodge, 46 Cromer Rd, ☎0263.720016, ⇌7.

NORTH WALSHAM:
Beechwood, 20 Cromer Rd, ☎0692.403231, ⇌11. Elderton Lodge, Thorpe Mkt, ☎0263.833547, ⇌7, ✿ ✕. Forest Edge, Mill Rd, Edingthorpe, ☎0692.500350, ⇌5. Ollands, Swanns Lake, Worstead, ☎0692.536640, ⇌3.

SANDRINGHAM:
Park House, ☎0485.543000, ⇌17, ✿ ✕ ☲ ⅙.

SEDGEFORD:
Dove Hill Cottage, ☎0485.71642, ⇌2.

SHERINGHAM:
Beacon, 1 Nelson Rd, ☎0263.822019. Crown Inn, The Promenade, ☎0263.823213. Fairlawns, 26 Hook Hill, ☎0263.824717. Highfield, 40 The Avenue, ☎0263.825524, ⇌3. Melrose, 9 Holway Rd, ☎0263.823299.

SNETTISHAM:
Compasses pub, 16 Lynn Rd, ☎0485.543270, ⇌3, ✕ ☲. Old Bakehouse, 2 Old Church Rd, ☎0485.541212, ⇌4, ✿ ⅙. Rose & Crown, Old Church Rd, ☎0485.541382, ⇌3, ✕ ☲ ⅙.

THORNHAM:
London Ho, Main Rd, ⇌. Orchard Ho, High St, ☎0485.26259, ⇌3.

TRUNCH:
Manor Farmhouse, Brewery Rd, ☎0263.720595, ⇌6.

WALSINGHAM:
Old Rectory, Waterden, ☎0328.823298, ⇌3.

WELLS-NEXT-THE-SEA:
Cobblers, Standard Rd, ☎0328.710155, ⇌8, ✕. Crown, The Buttlands, ☎0328.710209, ⇌15, ✕ ☲. Normans, Standard Rd, ☎0328.710657, ⇌7. Old Post Office, Warham, ☎0328.710547, ⇌4. Scarborough House, Clubbs La, ☎0328.710309, ⇌10. Well House, Standard Rd, ☎0328.710443, ⇌4. West End House, Dogger Lane, ☎0328.711190, ⇌4.

WOLFERTON:
Old Rectory, ☎0485.540496, ⇌3.

YOUTH HOSTELS:
Hunstanton, ☎0485.532061; King's Lynn, Thorseby College, College La, ☎0553.772461, 37 beds; Sheringham, ☎0263.823215.

CAMPING & CARAVAN SITES:
BACTON: Cable Gap Park, Coast Rd, ☎0692.650667, ⌖+▲ 27.
CROMER: Beeston Regis C & C Park, Cromer Rd, ☎0263.823614, ⌖20, ▲400. Forest Park, Northrepps Rd, ☎0263.513290, ⌖+▲429. Gap Caravan Site, Beach Rd, East Runton, ☎0263.513292, ⌖6. Laburnum Park, Water La, West Runton, ☎0263.75473, ⌖6. Manor Farm, East Runton, ☎0263.512858, ⌖+▲462. Roman Camp, West Runton, ☎0263.75256, ⌖11. Seacroft C & C Park, Runton Rd, ☎0263.511722, ⌖+▲118. Woodhill Park, Cromer Rd, East Runton, ☎0263.512242, ▲169 ⌖225.
FAKENHAM: Fakenham Racecourse C & C, ☎0328.862388, Apr-Sep, ⌖+▲ 150.

Crossways, Holt Rd, Lt Snoring, ✆0328.878335, 🚐+⛺26.
HUNSTANTON: Manor Park, Manor Rd, ✆.0485.532300, Apr-Oct. **Searles,** South Beach, ✆0485.534211, Mar-Sep.
KING'S LYNN: Great Ketlam Farm, Pentney, ✆0760.338797.
MUNDESLEY: Kiln Cliffs, Cromer Rd, ✆0263.720449,, 🚐3. **Links Park,** Heath Lane, ✆0263.720665, ⛺20 🚐30. **Sandy Gulls,** Cromer Rd, ✆0263.720513, 🚐40.
NORTH WALSHAM: Pampas Park, Old Yarmouth Rd, ✆0629.405829, 🚐+⛺50.
OVERSTRAND: Ivy Farm, Carr Lane, ✆0263.78239, 🚐20.
SHERINGHAM: Woodlands, Holt Rd, ✆0263.823802, 🚐300.
SNETTISHAM: Diglea, Beach Rd, ✆0485.541367, Mar-Oct.
STIFFKEY: High Sand Creek, ✆0328.830479, 🚐+⛺75.
WELLS: Pinewoods C & C Park, ✆0328.710439, ⛺200 🚐200.
WEYBOURNE: Kelling Heath, ✆0263.70224, 🚐+⛺30.
WIVETON: Long Furlong Cottage, Long Lane, ✆0263.740266, ⛺15 🚐14.

Swans enjoy the peaceful waters of Wells Harbour at high tide, particularly if there's food around.

KINGS and QUEENS of ENGLAND

from 1066 to 1901

1066–1087 **William I,** William the Conqueror, first of the Norman kings. At the end of his reign the Domesday Book is compiled, listing everything of value in the land.

1087–1100 **William II,** William Rufus.

1100–1135 **Henry I,** The Lion of Justice, younger brother of William II. Dies in Normandy.

1135–1154 **Stephen.**

1154–1189 **Henry II,** who rules most of the British Isles and half of France. Feudalism dies at the start of his reign.

1189–1199 **Richard I,** Richard the Lion-Heart or *Coeur de Lion,* goes on crusades and spends only months in England.

1199–1216 **John,** called 'Lackland' because he loses much of the French territory.

1216–1272 **Henry III,** crowned at the age of 10. In his reign Magna Carta becomes recognised as the law of the land.

1272–1307 **Edward I,** in whose reign wool becomes of major economic importance, particularly in East Anglia.

1307–1327 **Edward II,** elder son of Edward I. He is deposed in favour of his son and allegedly murdered with a red-hot poker in the anus.

1327–1377 **Edward III.** The French liaison is breaking down and in 1338 the Hundred Years War begins against France. The Black Death strikes in 1348. By 1375 England has lost all but a few towns in France.

1377–1399 **Richard II.** The first experiment with the poll tax results in the Peasants' Revolt of 1381.

1399–1413 **Henry IV,** with a weak claim to the throne, survives several battles but dies of an epileptic fit.

1413–1422 **Henry V,** who recovers some of the French provinces, dies from dysentery at Vincennes, aged 36.

1422–1461 **Henry VI** becomes king at the age of eight months. After Joan of Arc is burned at the stake the Earl of Suffolk proposes Henry marry Margaret of Anjou. In 1453 the king goes mad, shortly before the Wars of the Roses.

1461–1483 **Edward IV** succeeds from the deposed Henry while Lancaster and York continue to fight. Edward dies from pneumonia, aged 40.

1483 **Edward V** reigns from 9 April to 25 June but is victim of intrigue and dies, one of the 'princes in the Tower.'

1483–1485 **Richard III,** Edward's uncle, seizes the throne but dies at the Battle of Bosworth.

1485–1509 **Henry VII** brings in the Tudor dynasty and invades France yet again, while Columbus discovers America.

1509–1547 **Henry VIII,** the most outrageous king on the English throne, takes six wives. Because the Pope refuses to acknowledge divorce Henry breaks from the Catholic Church and Protestantism begins. Cardinal Wolsey of Ipswich is for a while the power behind the throne. Henry dies, aged 55, from problems with his leg.

1547–1553 **Edward VI,** Henry's only son becomes king. The peasants revolt again in Norfolk in 1549, and Edward dies of tuberculosis, aged 15.

1553 **Lady Jane Gray** is proclaimed queen on 6 July but loses her support on the 19th; she loses her head the next year.

1553–1558 **Mary I** becomes queen while staying at Framlingham Castle, Suffolk. She marries Philip of Spain who claims the English throne – unsuccessfully. Mary dies from flu.

1558–1603 **Elizabeth I**, Good Queen Bess, is probably England's most charismatic queen. In her reign Drake sails around the world and later defeats the Spanish Armada.

1603–1625 **James I,** who is James VI of Scotland, unites the two kingdoms. Guy Fawkes tries to blow up Parliament.

1625–1649 **Charles I.** Charles dismisses Parliament in 1629, but it grows strong and in 1642 the Civil War starts, Parliament versus the Crown. Charles is publicly beheaded at Whitehall and the Monarchy falls.

1649–1660 **The Commonwealth.** Oliver Cromwell becomes Lord Protector.

1660–1685 **Charles II,** son of the last king, regains the throne. The Plague strikes in 1665 and the Great Fire of London destroys the city in 1666. Charles dies of apoplexy, having secretly received the last rites of the Catholic Church.

1685–1689 **James II** encourages Catholicism but is overthrown by a Protestant revolution.

1689–1702 **William III and Mary II** are offered the throne, but a Protestant succession is demanded. Mary dies from smallpox in 1694 and William rules alone.

1702–1714 **Anne,** daughter of James II, satisfies the legal requirement and so reigns. The 1707 Act of Union legally binds England and Scotland.

1714–1727 **George I** ushers in the House of Hanover. Sir Robert Walpole creates the post of Prime Minister. George has a heart attack near Osnabrück, aged 67.

1727–1760 **George II.** Britain expands into North America and India.

1760–1820 **George III,** the longest-reigning king.

1820–1830 **George IV.** An unpopular monarch, George dies of liver failure after too much drinking.

1830–1837 **William IV** dies from the same cause, aged 71.

1837–1901 **Victoria,** grand-daughter of George III, is the longest-reigning monarch of all, coming to the throne aged 18.

And more royal signatures: Richard II (Le Roy R2); Henry IV (HR); Henry V (RH); James I; Charles I; Edward V (R. Edwardus Quintus).

INDEX

144